THE EXCAVATION OF HUMMINGBIRD SHELTER

BY

CARL E. CONNER

AND

DANNI L. LANGDON

COLORADO STATE OFFICE
BUREAU OF LAND MANAGEMENT
DENVER, COLORADO

1989

Designed By: Leigh Wellborn
Series Production: Frederic J. Athearn

FOREWORD

This volume represents the excavation of a rock shelter in the Craig, Colorado District. The results of the work are of value to archaeologists and the general public because this is one of the few excavations that has occurred in northwestern Colorado.

The information gathered by Carl Conner and Dani Langdon adds insight as to prehistoric peoples in the western part of Colorado while also providing habitation dates, along with an analysis of tools and materials that were used to sustain these ancient people.

Of equal interest is the fact that this excavation was sponsored by Beartooth Oil and Gas Company in response to a need to preserve historic data as part of an ongoing oil and gas operation near this site. The cooperation of Beartooth made this project possible. I am proud that public and private sector entities can work together in preserving our irreplaceable past.

I am pleased to make this volume available to both the professional community and to the general public in the hope that readers will find the information useful and of interest.

Neil F. Morck
State Director
Colorado

Table of Contents

List of Figures

List of Tables

Acknowledgements

Our sincere thanks go to Beartooth Oil & Gas Company, particularly their representative Ken Currey, for supporting the excavation of the Hummingbird Rockshelter.

Also, we are grateful to Curtis Martin, field supervisor and photographer, whose enthusiasm and energy matched those of the hummingbirds who visited the site throughout our stay.

Finally, we are appreciative of the guidance and assistance given us by BLM archaeologists Michael Pointkowski and Mike Selle. Thanks!

INTRODUCTION

In response to the U.S. Department of the Interior, Bureau of Land Management's (BLM) requirement that damages incurred by archaeological site 5RB1463--the Hummingbird Rockshelter--be mitigated, Beartooth Oil & Gas Company (Beartooth) of Billings, Montana, contracted Grand River Institute (GRI) to conduct test excavations at the site during the summer of 1985. Mitigation was required because of the violation of BLM Special Stipulation #17 that was attached to the APD filed by Beartooth for gas well Federal #20-3, which lies immediately adjacent to the archaeological resource.

Located in Little Bull Draw in Rio Blanco County, Colorado, approximately twenty miles south of Rangely, site 5RB1463 was initially recorded as a prehistoric rockshelter of unknown cultural affiliation. At the time of its documentation, it was undisturbed except by minimal natural erosion. Subsequent to the development of well #20-3, however, the site was vandalized, a pit approximately 1.5m square being dug in front of the rockshelter. Disturbance of the resource, on which a final determination of eligibility to the National Register of Historic Places (NRHP) had not been made, constituted a violation of the National Historic Preservation Act, Executive Order 11593, and the Archaeological Resources Protection Act.

The broad purposes of the testing were to mitigate the vandal's impacts to the site and to provide for a determination of no adverse effect as mandated by 36 CFR 800.4(c). Defining the extent of damage, the horizontal and vertical extent of the cultural deposits, and the nature of these deposits were the primary goals delineated in the scope of work.

Field work was conducted during the months of May and June, 1985. Principal Investigator for the project was Carl E. Conner; Project Archaeologist was Curtis W. Martin. Eddy Newcomb assisted in the field. Report preparation was the responsibility of Conner and Danni L. Langdon.

The study was conducted under Colorado BLM Antiquities Permit Number C-39291 in consultation with the Craig District and White River Area Offices of the BLM. Field notes and lithic artifacts recovered during the excavation will be housed in the curation facility of Mesa College, Grand Junction. Perishables will be housed at the Anasazi Heritage Center.

DESCRIPTION OF STUDY AREA

The Hummingbird Rockshelter (5RB1463) is located in northwestern Colorado within Little Bull Draw, an intermittent tributary of West Douglas Creek (Figure 1). The focus of the site is a shallow, south-facing overhang formed in a massive sandstone bed of the Mesaverde Group. The site occurs on a bench fifty feet above a small drainage at an elevation of 6240' (1902m) (Figures 2 and 3).

The surrounding terrain is characterized by shallow to deep arroyo-cut canyons and narrow, flat-topped ridges. Slopes are moderate to steep and are generally to the east toward Douglas Creek, a usually dependable source of water. The dominant topographic features of the landscape are Texas Mountain to the southwest and Cathedral Bluffs to the east. The White River lies eighteen miles distant, to the north.

Climatically, the area is characterized as a middle latitude arid steppe; sunshine is abundant during all seasons and annual precipitation is low. A BLM (1978) unit resource analysis for the Rangely Planning Unit records temperatures ranging from over 100°F during the summer months to -40°F in January and February. Precipitation averages 24.0-27.5cm annually with winter snowfall accounting for most of the moisture. A frost-free period of 140 days is the norm (Gordon et al. 1981:36).

Soils in the immediate site area are thin, sandy loams that have formed in residuum from sandstone bedrock decay. Some aeolian deposits of fine loess occur sporadically as well and have, in spots, accumulated to depths greater than 20cm. These soils support an Upper Sonoran vegetation community that is dominated by pinyon and juniper, with occurrences of sagebrush, mountain mahogany, bitterbrush, and grasses.

Wildlife inhabitants of the area include the mule deer, desert cottontail, other rodents, coyote, lizards and snakes, and a variety of birds--chukars, geese, ducks, doves, and numerous non-game species and raptors. The area is of particular importance to the mule deer as it falls within

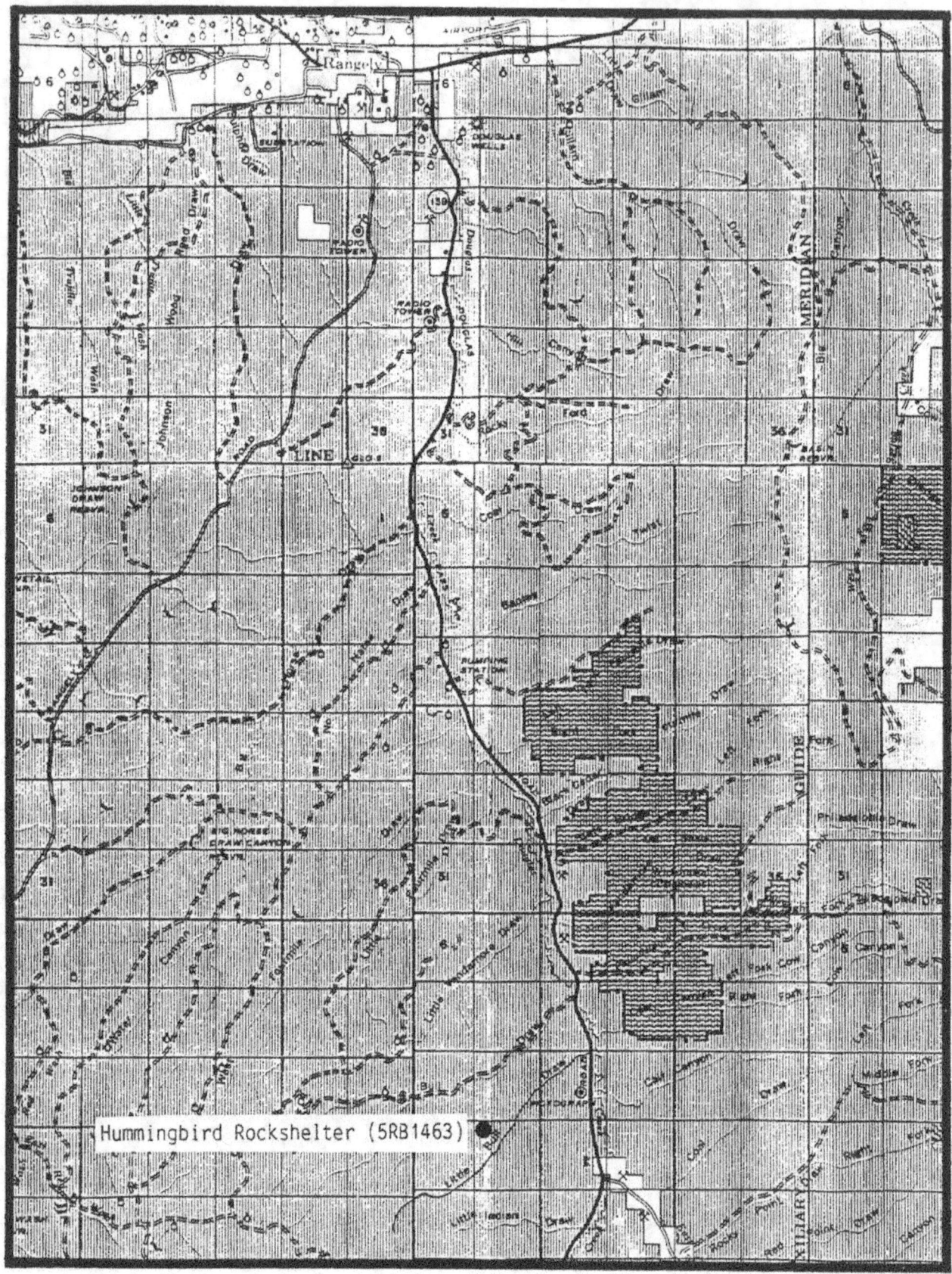

Figure 1. Area map showing location of the Hummingbird Rockshelter (site
5RB1463) in Rio Blanco County, Colorado.

-4-

Hummingbird Rockshelter, 5RB1463.

Upper photograph shows sandstone outcrop and pinyon-juniper bench within site area. View south.

Photograph at left shows first excavation unit (8N5W) within vandal's pit. View northeast along outcrop.

Figure 2.

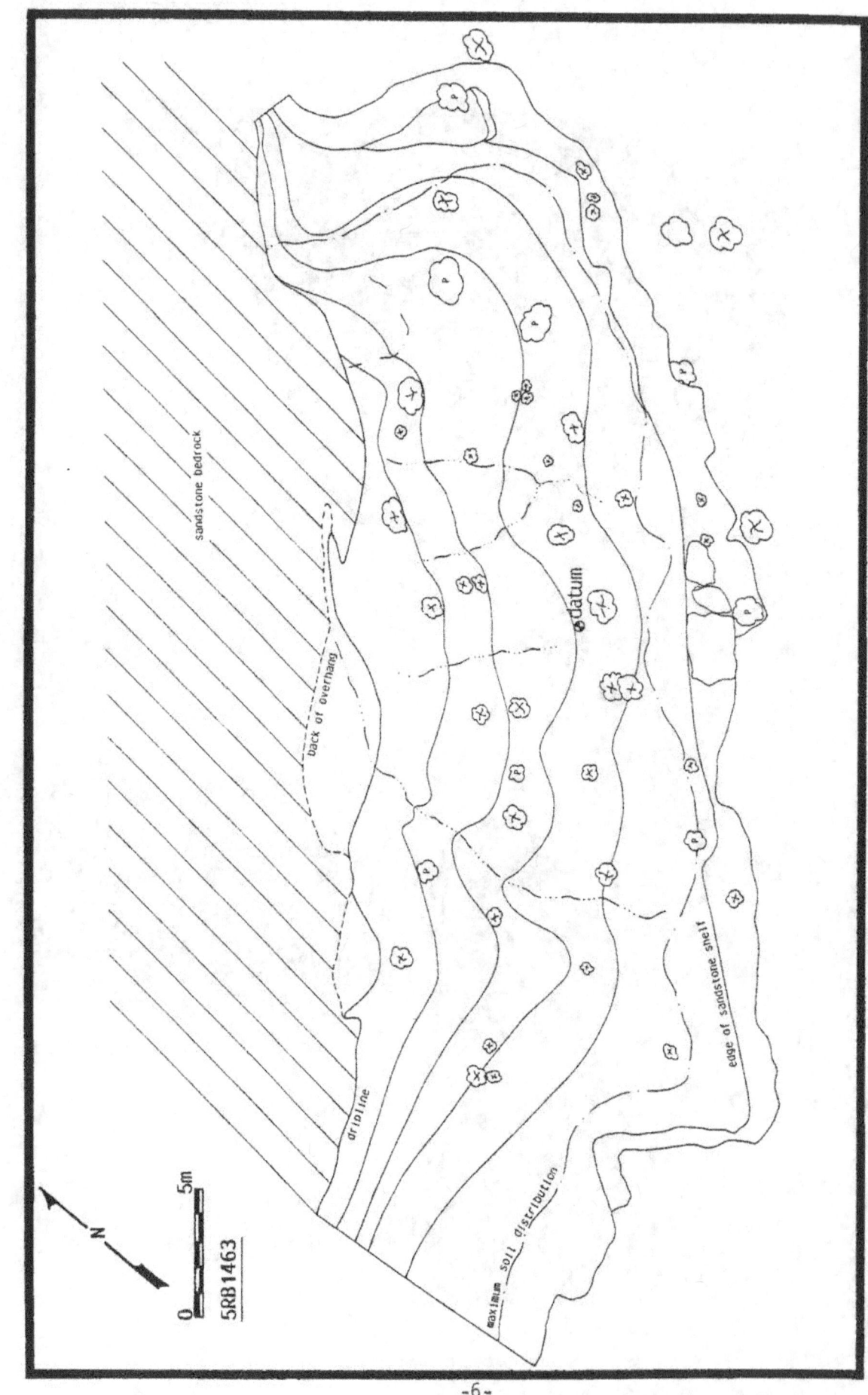

Figure 3. Contour map of the Hummingbird Rockshelter, site 5RB1463. Elevation 6240'. Contour interval one foot.

this mammal's winter range.

Paleoenvironmental data for the Colorado Plateau are scant, but it is generally agreed that conditions have remained fairly constant over the last 12,000 years and that any shifts in effective moisture and temperature have not been of a magnitude great enough to alter the area's classification as a steppe (Jennings 1978:12,15). Although there may have been minor fluctuations climatically, floral and faunal resources available prehistorically were probably those available today. Creasman's (1981) investigations in the Canyon Pintado district found evidence of fairly continuous occupation of the Douglas Creek area since 2750 B.C. (aside from a 75-year drought, A.D. 1225-1300), and it is presumed that resources exploited by succedent aboriginal populations remained much the same throughout this period.

OVERVIEW OF PREVIOUS ARCHAEOLOGICAL WORK

As emphasized by Grady (1984) in the Colorado Preservation Office's publication "Northwest Colorado Prehistoric Context," our knowledge of this area's prehistory is rather limited. Prior to 1973, few systematic archaeological studies had been conducted and most of what was "known" about the area was actually inferred from studies elsewhere. However, there were several important early investigations, among them the study of several Fremont sites in the Castle Park area and subsequent excavations from 1939 to 1941 by Charles R. Scoggin (report compiled by Robert F. Burgh 1948); the excavation of Hell's Midden (Castle Park) during 1948 and 1949, which revealed Fremont and Archaic components (Lister 1951); the 1964-65 excavations of several additional Fremont sites in Dinosaur National Monument by David Breternitz (1970); and the surveys in the Blue Mountain and Douglas Creek areas by Wenger (1956) which identified numerous Fremont and Ute sites.

In 1973, compliance with cultural preservation laws prompted the beginning of archaeological contract work in the area; since then, over 30 major survey projects have been completed. An inventory of the Sand Wash Basin by Richard Stucky (1977) produced evidence of human occupation since 8500 B.P. and recovered fifteen projectile points of PaleoIndian origin-- unusual points that suggest the possibility of a Middle PaleoIndian variant peculiar to the Western Slope (referred to as the Sand Wash Basin Type I). Similar point finds have been made in the Piceance Basin and near Grand Junction (Conner and Langdon 1980, Conner et al. 1980; and Martin et al. 1980). Other local studies have also produced evidence of recurrent occupation since the Middle PaleoIndian period. In their Class III inventory of 11,700 acres for the Texas-Missouri-Evacuation Creeks project, Gordon et al. (1981) documented Folsom, Agate Basin, and Hell Gap points, Early, Middle, and Late Archaic points, Fremont diagnostics, and Ute-Shoshonean artifacts. In Douglas Creek, test excavations of two sites in the Canyon Pintado Historic District in 1977-78 yielded materials associated with the Late Archaic and Fremont periods (Creasman 1981). Thus, though there are gaps in the data base, a cultural chronology has evolved for northwestern Colorado; a brief description of the major cultural/temporal periods follows.

Aside from the materials recovered by Stucky's Sand Wash study, the PaleoIndian period predating 5000 B.C. is represented by only a few surface finds in the lower reaches of the White River drainage (e.g. Dinosaur National Monument, Missouri Creek, the Piceance Basin, and the Moon Lake project areas [Gordon et al. 1981:35]), on Cross Mountain, and north of the Danforth Hills. Two Clovis points have been reported as surface finds from the Rangely area as well (Mike Selle, personal communication). All specimens appear similar to points of the Great Plains, suggesting a cultural connection during PaleoIndian times with Wyoming and areas south and east of the Rocky Mountains. The discovery of two partially fossilized bison bones of Paleo-Indian age that exhibited possible butchering marks provides further evidence of human occupation during these times (Gordon et al. 1981:35). In addition, a radiocarbon date of 9190±130 B.P. was obtained from a charcoal deposit in a buried stream channel eight meters deep in Douglas Creek alluvium (Creasman 1981:II-8). Unfortunately, the date was not associated with any diagnostic artifacts.

With the disappearance of the Pleistocene megafauna, there developed a lifestyle known as the Archaic, dependent upon the exploitation of varied floral and faunal resources. The Early Archaic period (5000-3000 B.C.) is poorly represented in northwestern Colorado; however, the Middle and Late Archaic periods are better documented (Grady 1984:31). This apparent disparity in material remains may relate to a population increase on the northern Colorado Plateau around 1000 B.C. - A.D. 400, as postulated by Madsen and Berry (1975:104). Such an increase may have occurred as a result of movement eastward from the northeastern Great Basin due to the extremely low water table there at that time (ibid.). This relatively dry paleoclimatic episode is thought to have persisted from around 500 B.C. to A.D. 500, the approximate beginning of the Fremont period.

The Fremont or Formative period (A.D. 400-1200) is associated with the emergence of horticulture, ceramics, and the bow and arrow. Because of the aridity and the marginal conditions of most of the uplands of northwestern Colorado in terms of horticultural possibilities, few areas show evidence of such practices and associated sedentary village life. The Canyon Pintado area, however, contains granaries, "tower structures," and Fremont-style ground stone, all suggestive of at least limited horticulture (Creasman 1981). Granaries have also been documented at Fremont sites in the Skull Creek and Blue Mountain areas. Elsewhere, Fremont-related rock art and projectile points are the only indicators of these peoples' presence; it is assumed they continued to pursue an Archaic subsistence pattern, practicing limited horticulture where possible.

Until very recently, it was believed that Fremont cultural traits disappeared in northwestern Colorado by about A.D. 1200. However, a carbon date of ca. A.D. 1450 from a tower structure near Dragon Trail may indicate a later occupation (personal communcation, Penny McPherson, 1984). In any case, it is generally agreed that Shoshonean speakers (Ute, Paiute, Shoshoni) were migrating into the Four Corners area by ca. A.D. 1200 (Smith 1974:16-17). Whether they were influential in the demise of the Fremont culture is unknown, but their strictly hunting-gathering subsistence may have exerted economic and environmental stress on their predecessors, Fremont or otherwise.

By 1776, Shoshoni groups were occupying the White and Yampa River basins, while the Utes inhabited lands south of the Grand (Colorado) River (Steward 1974:113). However, less than a century later, the Utes occupied all of western Colorado, having pressured the Shoshoni northward into Wyoming. Ute supremacy was short-lived, though; in 1881, the White River Utes, along with all others but the Southern Utes, were forced onto reservations in Utah, and western Colorado was opened to settlement.

FIELD METHODS

To fulfill the provisions of Special Stipulation #17 and to secure a determination of no adverse effect under regulation 36 CFR 800.4(c), the BLM proposed that a two-phase program of testing and data recovery be undertaken. The first phase was to entail a ten percent sampling of the estimated 800 square-meter site, the boundaries of which were defined in the Colorado Preservation Office (CPO) site inventory form of 21 April 1980. Forty of the 80 plots to be excavated in the first phase were to be statistically derived and valid (randomly selected). The remaining 40 squares of the ten percent sample were to be used to define features found during the sampling excavation, to open untested portions of the site, or to open a trench for profiling purposes. A second phase of the program (total excavation) was to be undertaken in the event that new research questions were generated that could not be answered from the data gathered during the first phase. However, it was recognized that phase I, by itself, could fulfill the criteria for a determination of no adverse effect.

Phase I was conducted in two stages. Stage I was effected to determine the nature and horizontal and vertical extent of the cultural deposits. First, a permanent datum was established and marked with a length of half-inch metal rebar driven into the ground near the central portion of the small bench, approximately five meters northwest of the bench's edge. Then, a one-meter continuous (Union) grid was laid out over the bench southeast of the overhang and sandstone outcrop. This area measured approximately 30m northeast-southwest and 12m northwest-southeast and encompassed about 360 m^2.

The grid system was laid at right angles to the edge of the bench and the sandstone outcrop, rather than aligning it with the cardinal directions. This procedure has been shown to greatly facilitate grid construction, excavation, and mapping procedures when working adjacent to rock outcrops or within overhangs. Thus, the grid system at Hummingbird was aligned roughly northwest-southeast, the "north-south" line running at 40° west of true north. For purposes of description in this report, when referring to the grid system, northwest (toward the back of the overhang) will be referred to as "north"; "south," "east," and "west" follow accordingly.

Units were selected for sampling according to a simple geometric design rather than using a statistically derived numbers table. This method was acceptable to the BLM and it both expedited the preliminary testing and ensured that all areas were sampled. As Redman (1975:150) points out:

> ...the sample which is simplest to lay out and most
> evenly dispersed is a systematic, or geometric design.
> Results of empirical and theoretical tests indicate
> that a systematic sample is not only simpler to per-
> form, but comes very close to an accurate estimate
> of the total population values.

The geometric pattern employed in stage I resulted in the opening of one-by-one-meter units every fifth meter across the length of the grid and every fourth meter along the north-south axis (Figure 4). Because the total site area was found to be only about 360 m^2 (as opposed to the originally estimated 800 m^2), twenty-one units (six percent of the site area) were designated for excavation during this test stage.

Stage II of phase I involved the excavation of an additional four percent of the site area, or another 14 units. These pits were clustered around grid squares excavated during stage I that produced the greatest artifact value, computed as follows:

Artifact	Value (per specimen)
Debitage	1
Patterned tool (chipped or ground stone)	5
Projectile point or ceramic sherd	10
Feature (non-portable artifact)	25

Thus, for example, a grid unit that produced five artifactual flakes, two tools, and a projectile point was assigned a total "artifact value" of 25. This system allowed stage II excavations to concentrate in the most

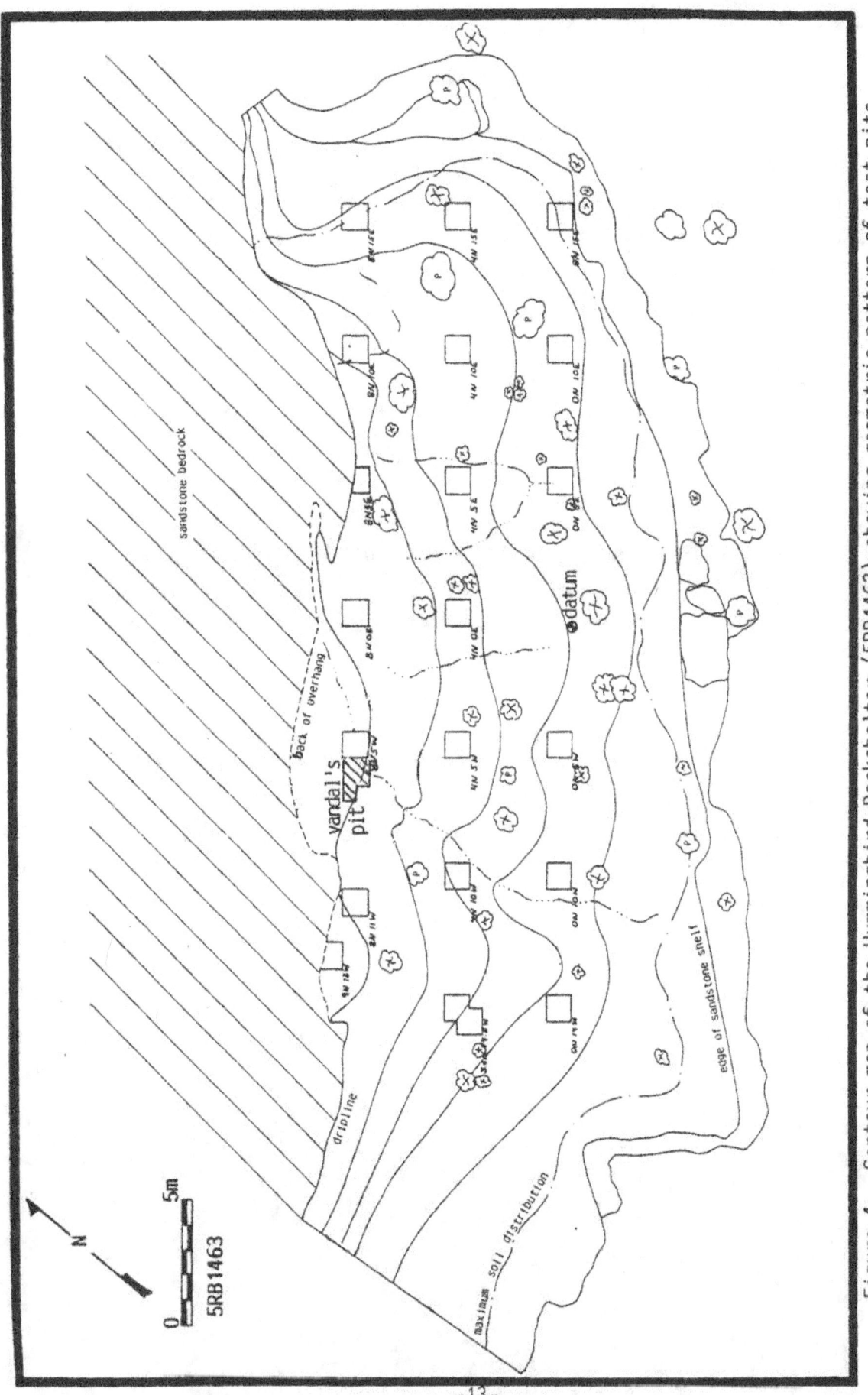

Figure 4. Contour map of the Hummingbird Rockshelter (5RB1463) showing geometric pattern of test pits excavated during Stage I.

productive areas of the site, maximizing data retrieval (Figure 5).

Units were excavated in arbitrary 10cm increments until natural or cultural stratigraphic levels were discovered, in which case these levels were adopted as the vertical control units. All units were cleared to a depth sufficient to determine that culturally sterile deposits had been contacted. Sub-sterile shovel tests were conducted to at least 10cm below the base of the lowest cultural deposits when suitably deep sediments were present. All fill was screened through 1/8" wire mesh shaker screens.

Records were maintained on each excavation unit and level. Features were mapped by unit (with plan and profile drawings) and excavated by halves. The fill from hearths was collected as a flotation sample, and radiocarbon, pollen, and archaeomagnetic samples were gathered as appropriate.

Artifacts and ancillary specimens were collected, numbered, and bagged separately by unit and level. Temporally and culturally diagnostic artifacts were numbered sequentially in the field and recorded by provenience. Profiles of unit walls were constructed and photographed (particularly features and stratigraphic variations).

Sufficient information had been gathered at the completion of phase I that phase II was obviated. Excavation units were therefore backfilled and the ground was smoothed to approximate the original surface.

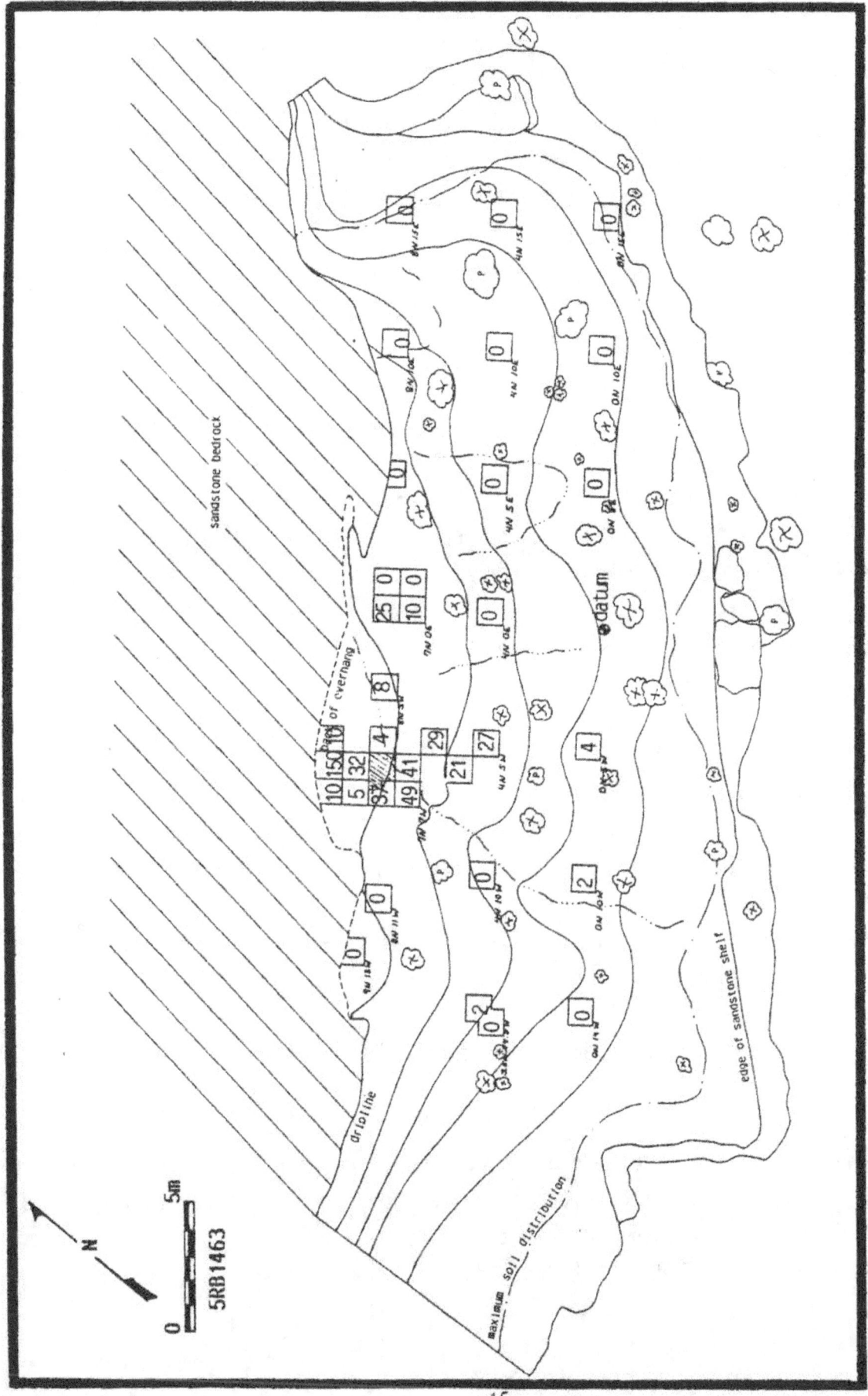

Figure 5. Contour map of the Hummingbird Rockshelter (5RB1463) showing the locations of all excavated units and their associated artifact values.

STRATIGRAPHY

Most of the site's cultural materials were concentrated immediately before the overhang in an area measuring approximately 10x7m. Within this zone, a 3x4m area proved to be the locality of greatest deposition and productivity, yielding the bulk of artifacts and, adjacent to the back wall, culturally stratified deposits. A natural depression in the sandstone bedrock here served to accumulate soils, ash, and charcoal to depths of 40-50cm (Figure 6).

While the fill of this 3x4m area rapidly became mixed away from the back wall (probably due to sheet washing) and distinct cultural levels were no longer visible, adjacent to the back wall a layer of uniformly cut and piled juniper bark strips (presumably from one occupation) provided an excellent reference level and allowed at least two cultural levels to be defined--the bark layer itself and that below. The discreteness of these two levels was confirmed through carbon dating--a date of A.D. 1010 ±60 being obtained for the bark layer and a date of A.D. 720±80 for that below.

Soils thinned considerably away from the site's center, particularly toward the east, the direction of upward incline of the sandstone bedrock. Soil depth measured only 3-10cm in the eastern portion of the overhang, yet a carbon sample extracted from a hearth in this area produced a date of 2220±90 B.P. (315±130 B.C.). Evidence of water erosion was observed here, and removal of more recent deposits is suspected.

Distinguishable stratigraphic units within the Hummingbird Rockshelter include:

Unit 1a - a light tan, loosely compacted, fine, sandy soil containing
cow dung and calcite (from the decomposing caliche layer below)
and found within the overhang. Thickness varies from 3.0cm to
16.0cm; thinning is to the east, as the bedrock slopes upward.

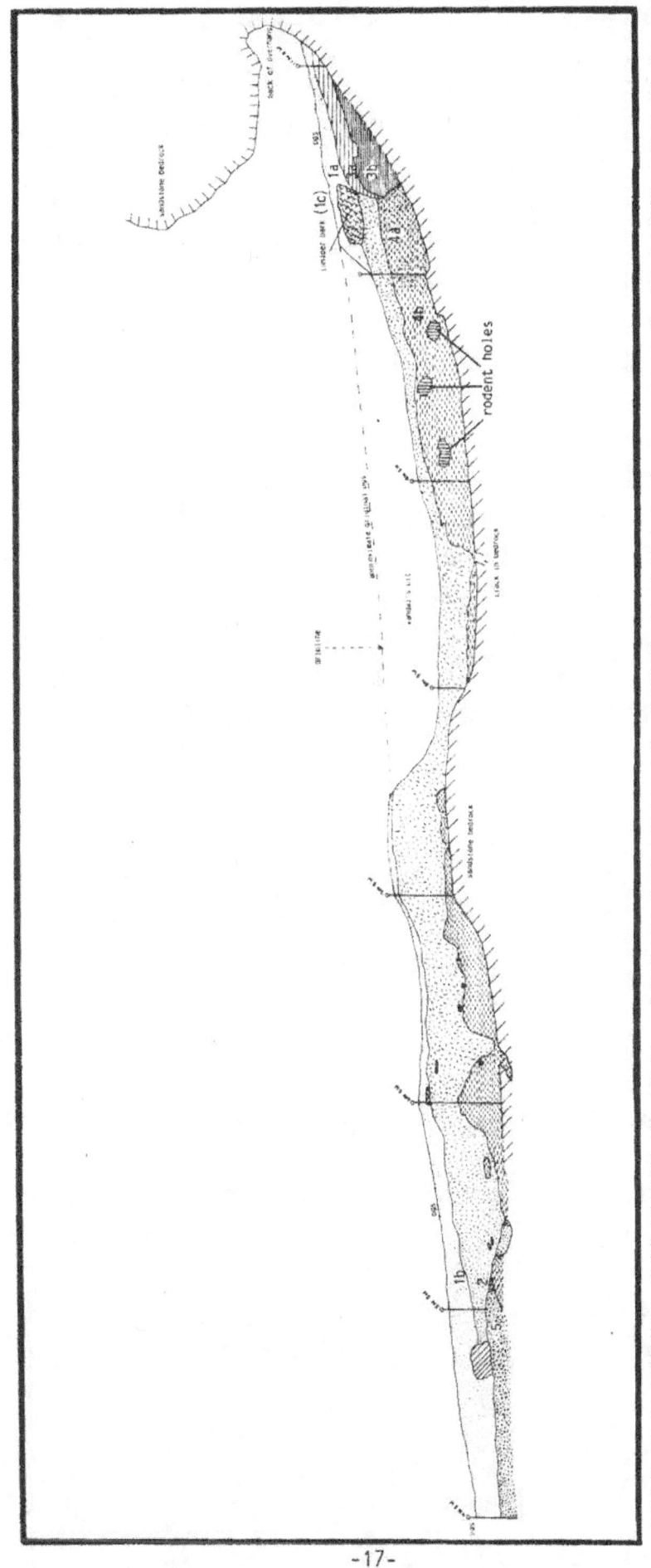

Figure 6. Profile along north-south grid line 5W, from 4N to 11N, within the Hummingbird Rockshelter. Stratigraphic units (1a, 1b, 1c, 2, 3a, 3b, 4a, 4b, and 5) are described in the text.

Unit 1b - a soil similar to 1a but without the dung and caliche. It
forms the topsoil of the bench; thickness ranges from 2.0 to
10.0cm.

Unit 1c - a soil similar to 1a but containing juniper bark as well.
(The bark was cut and stacked in the back of the overhang; presumably it was used in the making of cordage.) Occurring 2.0-
10.0cm below present ground surface (pgs), this level ranges in
thickness from 3.0 to 16.0cm. Most of the diagnostic artifacts
were recovered from this unit, which was radiocarbon dated at
940±50 B.P. (A.D. 1010±60) (Figure 7).

Unit 2 - a greyish-brown, ash-stained, sandy soil. Hardpacked and containing small concentrations and lenses of charcoal and dispersed
chunks of fire-reddened sandstone, this mixed layer has no dis-
cernible sublevels representing distinct cultural horizons. However, within the overhang and directly under Unit 1c, the upper
portion of this unit yielded a radiocarbon date of 1250±60 B.P.
(A.D. 720±80). Farther south, the unit becomes darker grey, al-
most black and contains large concentrations of charcoal; one
such concentration at 7N7W and 25-35cm below pgs produced a date
of 2000±60 B.P. (60±70 B.C.) (Figure 7).

Unit 3a - a soft, talc-like caliche layer. This loosely compacted
deposit occurs under the overhang directly above 3b. Thickness
of the unit is approximately 8cm.

Unit 3b - a hardened caliche layer. This layer lies directly atop
sandstone bedrock at the back of the overhang. Thickness
ranges from 1.0 to 20.0cm.

Unit 4a - a hard, sandy, light brown loam and decomposed sandstone
layer. This occurs atop sandstone bedrock, beneath the overhang.

Unit 4b - a soil similar to 4a but yellowish-tan in color and somewhat softer. This unit disappears 5m south of the overhang.

Unit 5 - a mottled grey clay. This layer is sterile and is found
fairly uniformly over the eastern and southern portions of the
site. Thickness varies from 10.0 to 30.0cm.

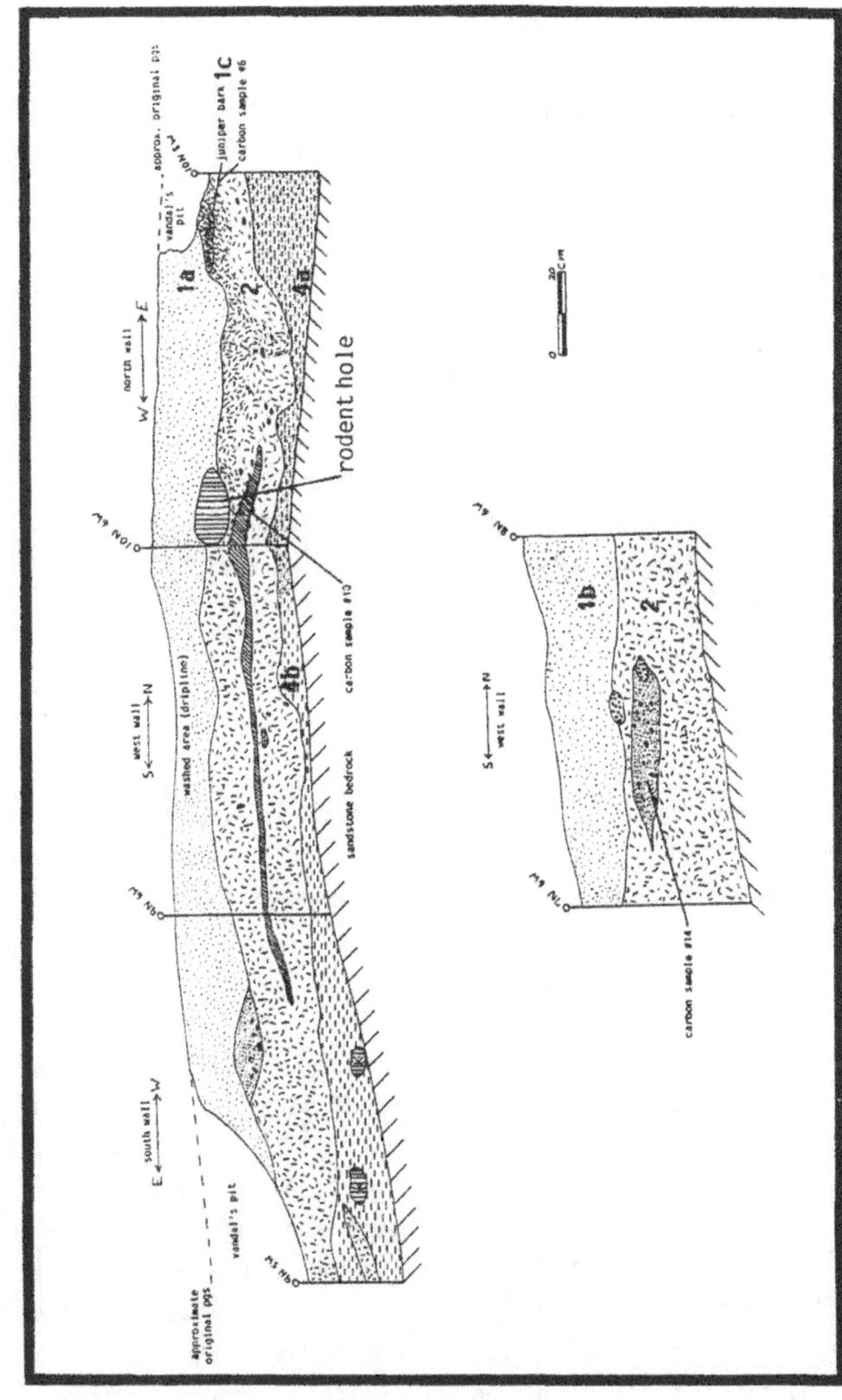

Figure 7. Profiles of excavation units 9N6W (north, west, and south walls) and 7N6W (west wall).

FEATURES

Two features were encountered during the excavation, a hearth at
8N0E and a stack of cut juniper bark strips at 10N6W. Associated radiocarbon samples produced dates of 2220±90 B.P. (315±130 B.C.) and 940±50
B.P. (A.D. 1010±60) for these features, respectively.

Located beneath 10-15cm of topsoil, Feature 1 was a shallow hearth
partially excavated into the deteriorating bedrock in the southeast corner of 8N0E (Figures 8 and 9). It measured 50-60cm in diameter and contained
about 5cm of ashy soils and sparse charcoal. The floor of the hearth
first appeared to be lined, but subsequent examination revealed only lay-
ered bedrock, broken and heat-reddened. Similar material was found around
the perimeter of the feature, and it is likely that bedrock layers were removed from the bottom to construct the sides. Several heat-reddened and
broken rocks lay atop the ashy soil in the northwest portion of the hearth;
these may have served as a griddle.

No diagnostic artifacts were located within the hearth. A projectile
point (a Rose Spring Corner-notched type) found in the northeast corner of
7N0E at 7cm below pgs was originally assumed to be temporally associated
with the hearth since the two were found in close proximity. However, in
light of the carbon date from the hearth, it is more probable that the
point represents a Fremont occupation of the site and the hearth is a mani-
festation of a Late Archaic occupation.

Feature 2 consisted of a pile of cut juniper bark stacked in the back
of the overhang, primarily in grid square 10N6W (Figures 10 and 11). The
feature measured approximately 110x60cm, was 5-20cm in thickness, and was
located 5-15cm below pgs. The bark was cut in fairly even strips measuring
about 25-35cm long and 3-5cm wide. A stick of juniper wood with a burnt
end was also retrieved from the pile. Perishable artifacts recovered from
the feature included four pieces of cordage, some twisted bark, and three
basketry items. One of the pieces of cordage (#25) is wrapped in a bundle
and is estimated to be 3m long; another (#34) is a segment of bow string;

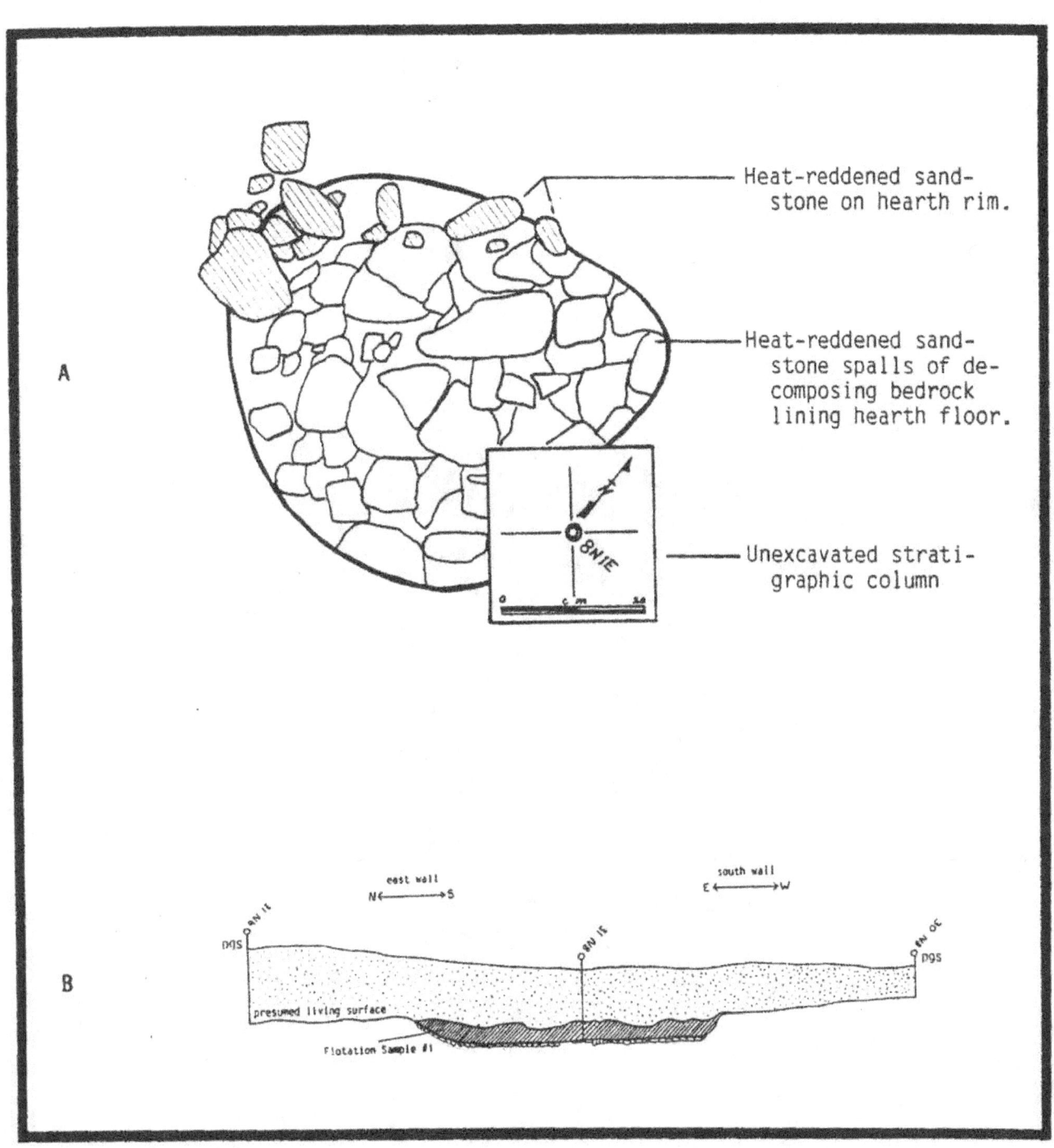

Heat-reddened sand-
stone on hearth rim.

Heat-reddened sand-
stone spalls of de-
composing bedrock
lining hearth floor.

Unexcavated strati-
graphic column

Figure 8. Feature 1, plan view (A) and profile (B).

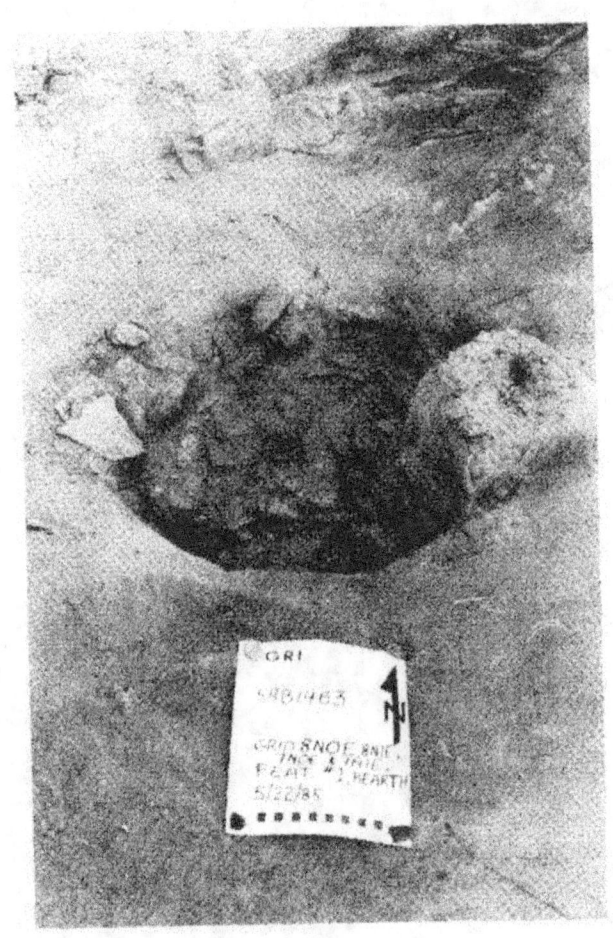

Figure 9. Photograph of Feature 1.

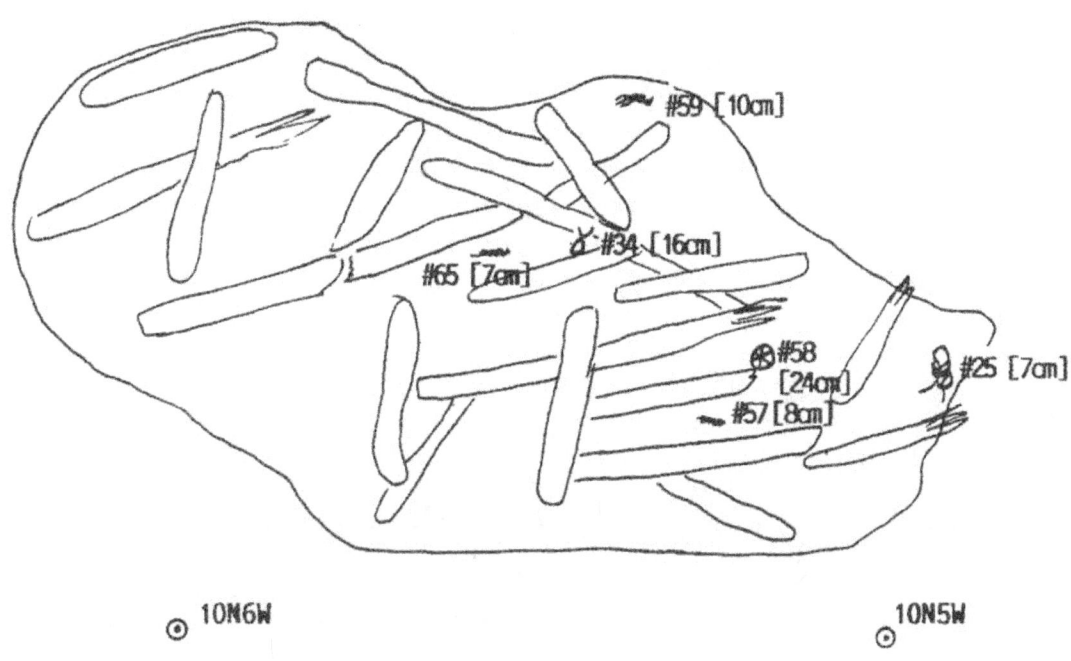

11N6W
⊙

11N5W
⊙

#59 [10cm]

#34 [16cm]

#65 [7cm]

#58
[24cm]

#25 [7cm]

#57 [8cm]

10N6W
⊙

10N5W
⊙

5RB1463
FEATURE 2

Figure 10.   Feature 2, plan view and photograph.   Plan view shows locations
             of textile artifacts within bark pile.

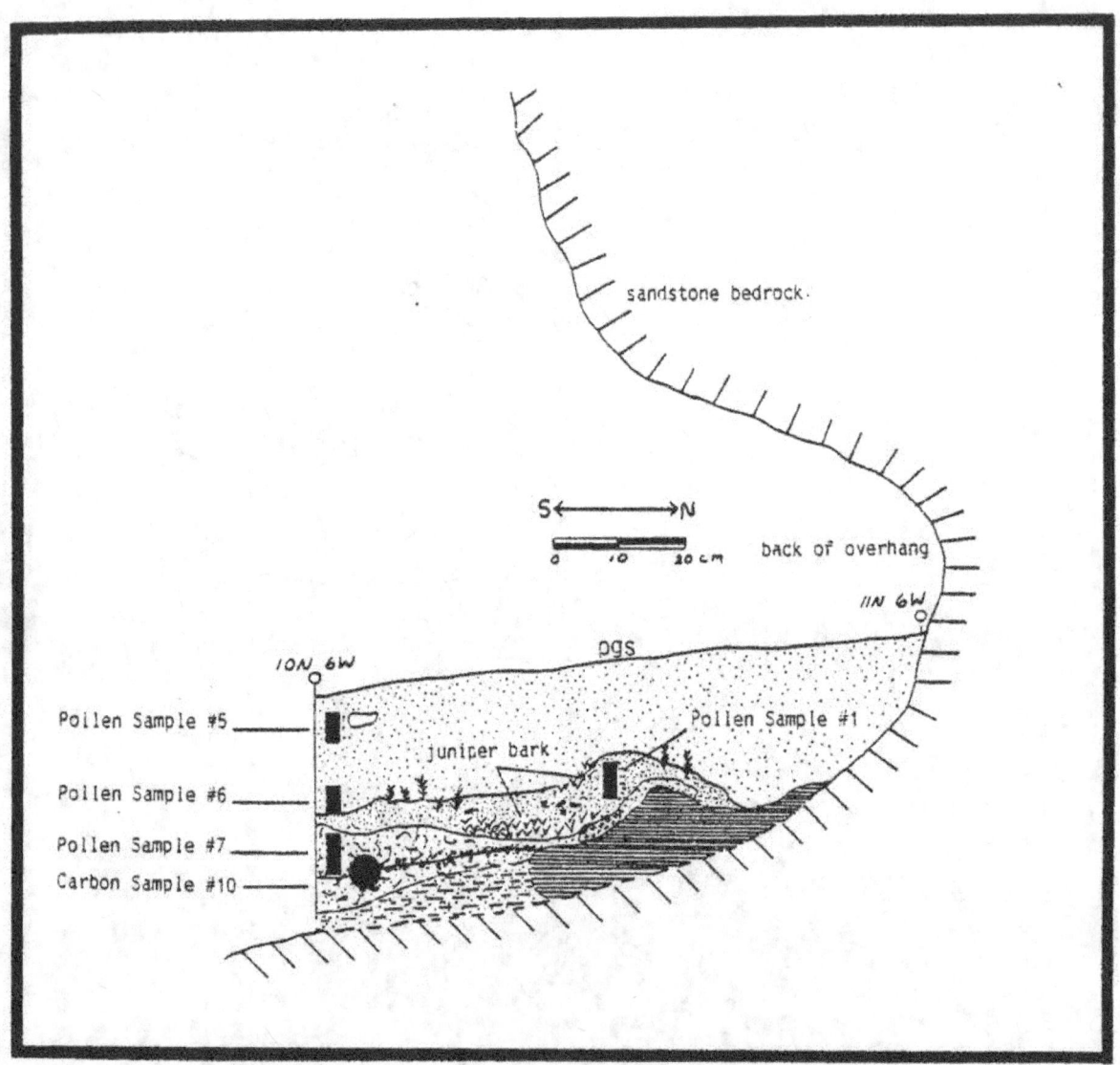

Figure 11. Profile of grid square 10N6W, west wall, showing Feature 2
(juniper bark pile) and associated stratigraphic levels.
Carbon sample #6 (not shown) was collected from Feature 2;
other carbon and pollen sample locations are indicated.

the third (#57) and fourth (#44a) are fragments of medium-diameter cordage. Among the basketry items are two fragments (#44b and #65) and a basket start (#58). A prehistoric work station is implied by the twisted bark (#59), a direct link between the raw materials and finished cordage found within Feature 2.

ARTIFACTS

Artifacts recovered during the excavation of Hummingbird Rockshelter were preliminarily sorted in the field as to type so that grid unit artifact values could be computed. Once in the laboratory, the few diagnostic specimens found were stylistically typed and compared with similar artifacts in the literature. Debitage was reexamined and sorted into finer categories, classified as to material, and measured. Biface thinning flakes were analyzed for tool function (cutting or scraping). Through this analysis, evidence of spatial use patterns or activity areas was sought; the use of statistics in this investigation was obviated by the concentration of artifacts in a very small area and the low number of artifacts present. Table I summarizes the artifacts recovered.

Table I. Artifact Summary	
Chipped Stone	
Projectile points	3
Other bifaces (fragments)	3
Debitage	
Primary flakes	3
Secondary flakes	19
Interior flakes	154
Chunks	31
Hammerstone	1
Ground Stone (fragments)	5
Bone (polished fragment)	1
Perishables	
Basketry	
Start (coiled)	1
Fragments	2
Cordage	
Knotted length	1
Bow string	1
Fragments	2
Twisted bark	1
Leather fragment	1

Chipped Stone

Three artifacts were functionally classified as projectile points or fragments thereof: #22, #33, and #42 (Figure 12). Other bifaces included

Artifact No. 5RB1463.22

Provenience: 7N0E, NE¼; 7cm below pgs
Type: Medium corner-notched projectile point
Material: Purplish chalcedony
Blade Outline: Straight to slightly excurvate
Shoulders: Right angle
Stem: Slightly expanding
Base: Expanding with obtuse angle of intersection with stem
Transverse Section: Plano-convex
Longitudinal Section: Plano-plano
Flake Blank Orientation: Proximal
Flaking: Irregular pressure and fine pressure retouch
Comparison/Comment: Rose Spring Corner-notched type, A.D. 300-950 (Holmer and Weder
    1980:56-60). Probably associated with early Fremont occupation of site (radio-
    carbon date of A.D. 720±80).

L=2.74cm
W=1.45cm
Th=0.32cm

Artifact No. 5RB1463.33

L=0.70cm
W=1.38cm
Th=0.29cm

Provenience: 7N6W; 24cm below pgs
Type: Large corner-notched projectile point base
Material: Pink-grey mottled chert
Base: Expanding
Comparison/Comment: Late Archaic Corner-notched, ca. 1000 B.C.- A.D. 500 (Frison
    1978:56-58; and Gooding 1981:28-29). Associated with Soil Level 2, carbon dated
    at 60±70 B.C.

Artifact No. 5RB1463.42

Provenience: 7N6W, SW¼; 19cm below pgs
Type: Large corner-notched projectile point base
Material: Reddish brown chert (heat-treated)
Shoulders: Acute
Stem: Slightly expanding
Base: Expanding
Transverse Section: Convex-convex
Flaking: Irregular pressure
Comparison/Comment: Late Archaic Corner-notched, ca. 1000 B.C. - A.D. 500 (Frison
    1978:56-58; and Gooding 1981:28-29). Although fragmentary, the point resembles
    the Pelican Lake type which was widespread over the northern and northwestern
    Plains area. Specimen was found associated with dark ashy and charcoal-stained
    soil level (Level 2), which carbon dated to 60±70 B.C. Chert source was probably
    Weaver Ridge.

L=1.50cm
W=1.89cm
Th=0.39cm

Figure 12. Projectile points, Hummingbird Rockshelter.

a bifacially worked edge, a fragment of a base, and a tip (part of a stone awl or drill). Except for a hammerstone, no other stone tools (including utilized flakes) were identified.

Debitage was scant. Only 207 flakes were recovered, most of them small. Of those classified as interior, 16 were biface thinning or re-sharpening flakes--indicative of tool revitalization. That most of the flakes were small secondary or tertiary types also suggests final preparation of stone tools. The debitage is summarized in Table II.

Type	Number	Chalcedony	Chert	Quartzite	Basalt	Siltstone
Primary	3(1.4%)		3			
Secondary	19(9.2%)	1	17	1		
Interior	154(74.4%)	13	133	6	1	1
Chunk	31(15.0%)	1	1	28	1	---
	207(100%)	15 (7.2%)	154(74.4%)	35(17.0%)	2(1.0%)	1(0.4%)

Table II. Debitage Summary

Sizes: Small (0-10mm) -143
       Medium (10-20mm) - 49
       Large (20+mm) - 15

Ground Stone and Bone

Only small fragments of grinding stones were recovered; none was recognizable as a specific tool. One piece of polished, burnt bone was identified as a possible bead fragment (5RB1463.10).

Perishables

Probably the most interesting and scientifically valuable finds were made while excavating the bark pile, Feature 2. Here, three pieces of basketry, four pieces of cordage, and pieces of twisted bark were recovered.

Basketry

Prior to the excavation of the Hummingbird Rockshelter, only two basketry finds had been reported from the area, one a shallow bowl or tray

from the West Douglas Creek area and the other a large, coiled storage or
carrying basket from the Texas-Missouri Creek drainage. The former was
removed by a vandal before BLM excavation could take place; the latter was
a surface find made by a local resident and reported to the BLM, who submitted it to the Anasazi Heritage Center for restoration and curation.
(The perishables from 5RB1463 will be conserved at the same facility.)
The basketry found at the Hummingbird Rockshelter is the only basketry
known from the area to have been recovered through scientific method.

Three basketry items were found at the site, all within Feature 2,
the bark pile (Figure 13). Two were found in the debris on and within the
pile, while the third, a basket start, was recovered from the bottom of
the pile. The first two are problematic artifacts: 5RB1463.65 is a single
split rod (8cm in length) with a double stick wrapping (both elements apparently of willow), and 5RB1463.44b is a very small segment of wrapping,
probably discarded or broken from an older basket.

The basketry start (5RB1463.58) is close coiled and has a half-rod
and welt (or two half-rods) stacked foundation. It is a normal or continuous coiled center with an interlocking stitch encircling the foundation, worked from right to left. The final form can only be speculated
upon, but the start appears to have been worked on the concave surface
and may be the beginnings of a shallow bowl or flat tray (Adovasio 1980:37).
Both the rods and stitching are willow (Salix).

An attribute analysis of the basket start shows it to be quite similar to Fremont types described by Adovasio (ibid.). The associated radiocarbon date (from the bark pile) of A.D. 1010±60 falls a little later than
the last occurrence of coiled basketry in the Uinta area, ca. A.D. 950;
however, it does occur within the period of Fremont use of this type of
basketry, ca. A.D. 400 to 1300. After A.D. 1300, the coiled basketry in-
dustry disappeared or was replaced by Numic techniques (ibid:39).

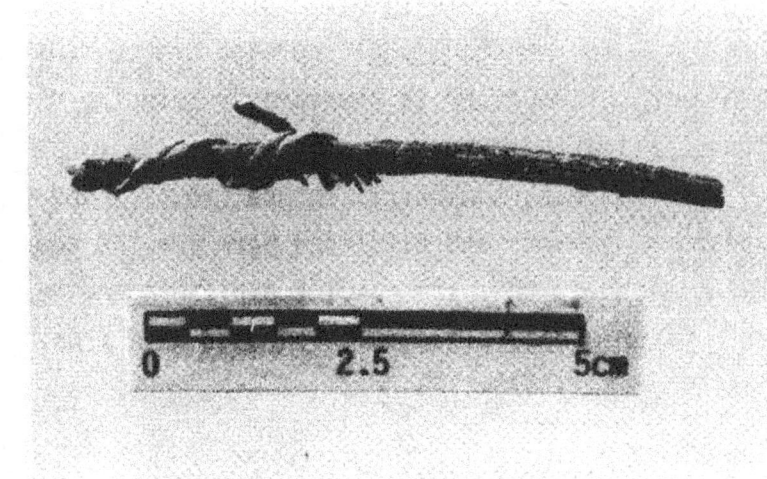

A

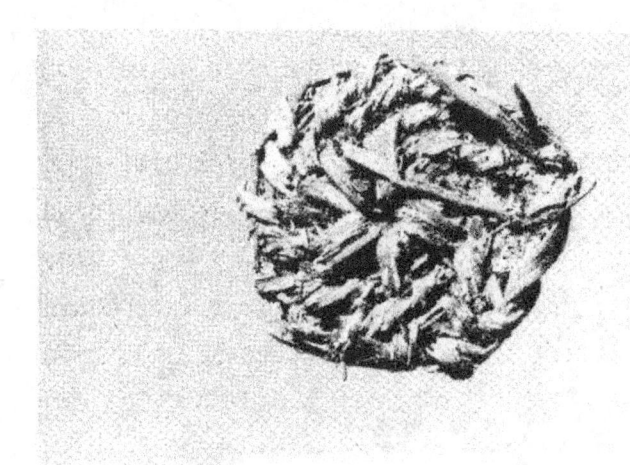

B

Figure 13. Basketry artifacts from Feature 2, dating A.D. 1010±60:
A) 5RB1463.65 - single split rod with double stick wrapping;
B) 5RB1463.58 - basketry start.

Cordage

An essential item to the aboriginal, cordage can be constructed from several common plants. Fine fiber is provided by stinging nettle, milkweed, and dogbane. Slightly coarser types of fiber are those gleaned from the thornapple, willow, rose, snowberry, spruce (roots), and elm bushes and trees. Sagebrush, juniper and cliffrose bark are the coarsest and weakest materials, although they are readily available and have a wide variety of uses. Of unequaled strength is cordage made from the long tendons of animals (Olsen 1973:136-137).

The first piece of cordage (5RB1463.25) encountered during the excavation is made of juniper bark and measures about 40cm long. This piece was produced using the 'quick' method described by Olsen (ibid.). Here, a single strand is pieced together with one end held in the left hand while the right hand either twists the strand clockwise or rolls it against the thigh out toward the knee. When enough has been pieced and rolled tight to a reasonable length--one that can be held between outstretched hands--the middle is grasped by the teeth and the two ends are brought together. The middle is then dropped and a counterclockwise motion automatically twines the two lengths together. This method forms a two-ply piece having a "z" twist. (The opposite procedure would produce an "s" twist of a two-ply cord.) Because of the fold, it is necessary to knot only one end. Indeed, artifact #25 has an overhand knot tied at one end and a loop (fold) at the other. It measures 0.3 to 0.5cm in diameter and has been folded twice and knotted in an overhand knot to form a small, easy-to-handle bundle. This length of cordage was found at the southeastern edge of Feature 2, the bark pile. (See Figure 14a.)

Four smaller pieces of cordage were found on or within the bark pile, along with juniper fibers that had been stripped from the bark and twisted together in bunches of varying diameters. Two of the cordage pieces are of the same type and probably represent a single artifact; they are combined as 5RB1463.34. The two segments, 9.0 and 6.5cm in length, are

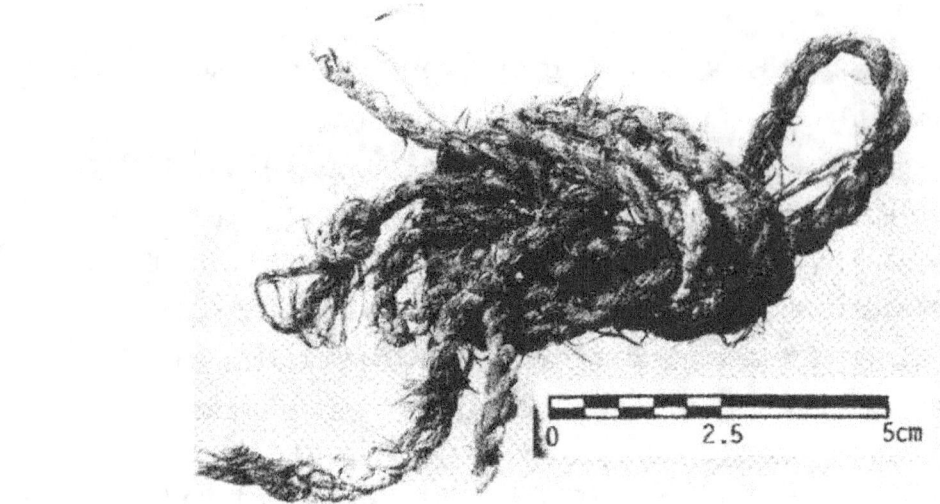

A

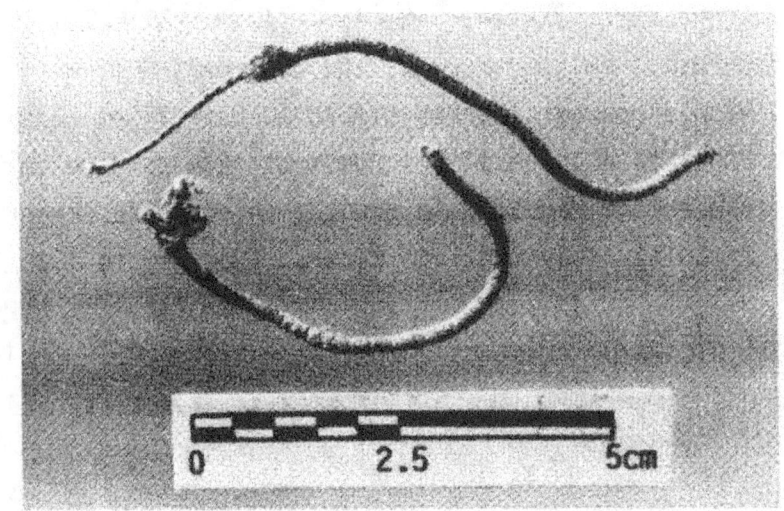

B

Figure 14. Cordage artifacts from Feature 2, dating A.D. 1010±60:
A) 5RB1463.25 - two-ply, z-twist cord of juniper bark;
B) 5RB1463.34 - segments of bow string.

constructed of two, two-ply s-twist cords, each cord about 0.07cm in diameter. Around a central cord the other is tightly wound--not twisted--in
a counterclockwise direction to form a string 0.17cm in diameter. A fine,
strong fiber (probably dogbane) was used to make this artifact, which was
likely employed as a bowstring. (See Figure 14b.)

The third piece of cordage, a small two-ply s-twist fragment
(5RB1463.44a), was found when sorting through the miscellaneous materials
found on or in the bark pile. The 4.5cm length has a diameter of 0.15cm
and is composed of fine, strong fiber.

The fourth piece of cordage, 5RB1463.57, is again a small piece measuring only 4.0cm long. It consists of two strands--the first a thick,
single ply piece of juniper or sage fiber (0.35cm in diameter) twisted
counterclockwise, the second a thinner, two-ply strand (0.15cm in diameter),
also twisted counterclockwise. The two are twined together in a clockwise
direction to form s-twist cordage. The combination of a fine, strong, two-
ply strand with a coarser, weaker strand of bark fiber results in a cord
that is stronger than an equal thickness of bark cordage but much more
sparing of the energy required to produce an equal thickness of stronger
but more difficultly acquired fine fiber. (See Figure 15a.)

Several pieces of twisted juniper bark fiber (#59) were found in Feature 2. These occurred in bunches of varying diameters. (See Figure 15b.)

Leather Fragment

A very small (2.5x1.0cm) fragment of still-pliable leather was found
atop Feature 2. Its small size and single cut edge suggest that it was
probably waste material.

A

B

Figure 15. Cordage and twisted bark from Feature 2, dating A.D. 1010±60:
A) 5RB1463.57 - s-twist cordage fragment;
B) 5RB1463.59 - twisted bark.

ANCILLARY SPECIMEN ANALYSES

Ancillary specimens were sought to try to date the site's cultural levels, to acquire information regarding paleoenvironmental conditions, and to determine economic activities of the site's occupants. Archaeo-magnetic and C-14 samples, pollen samples, and flotation, faunal, and floral samples were collected.

Dating (Radiocarbon and Archaeomagnetic Samples Processing)

Seventeen radiocarbon samples were gathered during excavation of the site; four obtained from different stratigraphic levels and features were processed to establish a cultural chronology. (One archaeomagnetic sample was taken from Feature 1 as well, but it proved to be unusable because the hearth had no clay collar and the soils lacked sufficient clay material to obtain a magnetized sample. [See Appendix A.]) Table III lists the carbon samples collected from the site; an asterisk indicates that the sample was submitted to Beta-Analytic of Coral Gables, Florida, for processing.

Table III. List of Carbon Samples and Proveniences		
Sample #	Field #	Provenience
*0	7A	8N0E, Feature 1 fill
1	13	9N6W, 20-30cm, center of N wall
2	16	9N6W, 30-40cm, S half
3	20	8N1E, 10-20cm, above living surface
4	27	10N5W, 1-30cm, screen sample
5	28	7N6W, 1-14cm, screen sample
*6	47	10N6W, 12cm, Feature 2
7	48	7N6W, 10-45cm, Strat. Unit 2
8	60	10N6W, 7-20cm, charcoal concen.
9	61	10N6W, 18-23cm, SW¼
*10	62	10N6W, 20-33cm, SW¼
11	64	10N6W, 5-33cm, Feature 2
12	35	7N6W, 11-18cm (burnt log)
13	36	7N6W, 1-40cm, screen sample
*14	74	7N7W, 25-35cm, charcoal lens
15	77	10N7W, 5-26cm, E½
16	81	10N6W, in/below bark & charcoal
17	83	8N0E, float from Feature 1 fill

*Asterisk indicates sample was processed.

Each of the four charcoal samples submitted was sufficient for processing, although sample #0 from Feature 1 was small, resulting in a relatively
large sigma (σ). Table IV lists the dates obtained and gives the calen-
dar years as corrected using Damon et al. (1974). The corrected dates and
sigmas are rounded to the nearest half decade.

Table IV. Dating Analysis from Charcoal Samples			
Sample #	Lab #	C-14 Age (years B.P. ± 1σ)	Calendar Years
5RB1463#0	Beta-13039	2220±90	315±130 B.C.
5RB1463#6	Beta-13040	940±50	A.D. 1010±60
5RB1463#10	Beta-13041	1250±60	A.D. 720±80
5RB1463#14	Beta-13042	2000±60	60±70 B.C.

The dates nearest one another were tested for contemporaneity using
the statistical t-test suggested by Long and Rippeteau (1973). Samples #6
and #10 demonstrated a less than one percent probability of being contemporaneous, while samples #0 and #14 showed an eight percent probability.
The latter two were then averaged by weighting the samples according to the
values of their corrected sigmas (ibid.). A date of 155±65 B.C. resulted.

The sequence of dates appears to be in order in terms of relative
stratigraphic position and occurrence of associated diagnostic artifacts.
The dates imply recurrent use of the site during the Late Archaic and Fremont periods.

Pollen Analysis

Seven pollen samples were taken at the site, five of which were sent
to Linda Scott of Palynological Analysts, Golden, Colorado, for analysis.
A list of these samples and their proveniences is provided in Table V (following page); an asterisk denotes the sample was analyzed.

Expectably large frequencies of both Juniperus and Pinus pollen were
evident in samples #2 (present ground surface) and #5 (just below present

```
+-----------------------------------------------------------+
|         Table V.  List of Pollen Samples and Proveniences |
|                                                           |
|    Sample #                  Provenience                  |
|                                                           |
|      *1        10N6W, Unit 1c, 17-22cm, bark layer, W wall |
|      *2        3N2E, present ground surface               |
|       3        8N6W, Unit 1b, 1-6cm, strat. block         |
|      *4        8N6W, Unit 2, 28-36cm, strat. block        |
|      *5        10N6W, Unit 1a, 3-8cm, strat. block        |
|       6        10N6W, Unit 1a, 15-19cm, strat. block      |
|      *7        10N6W, Unit 2, 22-29cm, strat. block       |
|                                                           |
|         *Asterisk indicates sample was processed.         |
+-----------------------------------------------------------+
```

ground surface). In contrast, the cultural samples--#1 (late Fremont),
#4 (Late Archaic), and #7 (early Fremont)--all showed a decrease in arbore-
al pollen but a notable increase in Cheno-ams (goosefoot and pigweed).

Samples #1 and #7 contained pollen more similar to one another than to
either of the samples from the modern community, although sample #1 (late
Fremont) exhibited a greater quantity of juniper pollen and a lesser quantity
of pine pollen than did sample #7 (early Fremont). The large quantity of
pine pollen observed in sample #7 corresponds well to dated levels elsewhere in the Douglas Creek drainage, for example, Vandamore Draw (A.D.780)
(Scott 1983) and Brady and Dripping Brow Cave Sites (A.D. 850) (Creasman
1981:IV-41,86).

Sample #4 (Late Archaic) contained less arboreal pollen than either
of the Fremont samples, the difference being primarily in the quantity of
pine pollen. Elevated frequencies of Graminae (grass) and High-spine Compositae (e.g. sunflower) pollen were also observed in this sample.

Faunal and Floral Analyses

Faunal samples were sent to analyst Elaine Anderson of Denver, Colorado. Microfloral (flotation) samples from Feature 1 and macrofloral samples picked from Feature 2 were analyzed by Lester Wheeler of Mesa, Colorado.

Faunal samples were scarce; of the few pieces recovered, most are presumed to be culturally unassociated. Unburned cottontail, white-tailed prairie dog, toad, and lizard bones and snail shells probably indicate intrusions into the cultural layers or deposits from carnivores who occupied the shelter when humans did not. Inspection of dung specimens revealed that not only had coyotes occupied the overhang sometime in the past and consumed rabbits, but that deer, domestic sheep, and cattle had apparently sheltered here as well. The few burned specimens excavated from the site were identified as cottontail (Sylvilagus sp.); these were recovered from all levels.

Flotation samples extracted from Feature 1 were dry screened to remove large specimens and gravel and then floated in tap water. The surface float was skimmed and dried, while the sediments were dried and sieved for organic materials. The dried organic materials were then examined using 20x magnification. Unfortunately, the fine ash of Feature 1 produced no seeds or identifiable plant or animal specimens.

Identifiable specimens from Feature 2 included twisted juniper bark, fragments of willow (Salix), and pine pitch. The lumps of pine pitch were of sufficient size and number to argue for their human importation.

Appendixes B, C, and D provide the reports of Beta-Analytic (C-14 processing), Linda Scott (pollen analysis), and Elaine Anderson (faunal identification).

DISCUSSION

Though small in area and previously disturbed by vandalism, the Hummingbird Rockshelter yielded significant cultural materials of uniqueness and diversity--materials that allow not only an occupational sequence to be defined but valid inferences to be made about the lifeways of the site's prehistoric occupants. Artifacts and features were few, yet among them were diagnostic projectile points and perishables in datable contexts (uncommon in the Douglas Creek area), as well as indicators of site-specific activities. Valuable ancillary specimens were obtained from the site, and their analyses provided evidence of similarities and differences in subsistence strategies and resource use among various occupant groups. Too, the radiocarbon and pollen sequences have permitted an interpretation of local paleoclimatic conditions and comparison with regional paleoenvironmental models from the Douglas Creek area and, more broadly, the southern Colorado Plateau. Overall, the findings at Hummingbird Rockshelter fit well into the prehistoric framework of northwestern Colorado and help to refine the established cultural sequence.

Cultural Chronolgy and Subsistence Strategies

The analysis of diagnostic artifacts and an audit of associated radiocarbon dates resulted in the identification of at least three distinct periods of use at the site. The earliest occupation directly associated with diagnostic artifacts (60±70 B.C.) falls within the Late Archaic horizon and is represented artifactually by a large, corner-notched projectile point base of the Pelican Lake type. Such points are commonly associated with Late Archaic occupation of the northwest Plains, and an influence from this area may be indicated. (A second, somewhat older Late Archaic occupation may be suggested by an isolated hearth [Feature 1] that dated to 315± 130 B.C.; however, this date did show an eight percent probability of being contemporaneous with the later Archaic sample and, thus, may not imply a separate occupation.) Early Fremont use of the site is indicated by a date of A.D. 720±80, obtained from charcoal deposits underlying Feature 2, the bark pile. A Rose Spring Corner-notched projectile point found several centimeters above Feature 1 may be related to this early Fremont level; such points are commonly found in Fremont contexts in Utah and Colorado dating from as early as A.D. 300 (Holmer and Weder 1980:59). Late Fremont use of the site is concluded from a date of A.D. 1010±60 and associated basketry items that comparatively type as Fremont. The basketry suggests influence from the Uinta region of Utah (Adovasio 1980:39).

Thus, recurrent use of the Hummingbird Rockshelter is clear. No evidence of successive use was found, however, and no cultural interface(s) were apparent.

Activities represented by the site's cultural manifestations include hunting and game processing, hide working, floral food processing, cooking, tool refinement and/or repair, and the manufacture of textiles. The small size of the site, the few scattered charcoal concentrations, and the paucity of debitage together suggest that the rockshelter served recurrently as a temporary--perhaps seasonal--campsite for a few individuals engaged in the exploitation of local natural resources. Excepting the evidence of textile manufacture in the late Fremont level, the subsistence strategies of the various occupations were probably much the same; the cultural levels evidenced fairly uniform tool associations and similar pollen assemblages.

The use of Hummingbird Rockshelter during late Fremont times as a textile workshop is assumed from the contents of Feature 2, a deliberate stash of cut juniper bark strips occurring within the most recent cultural level (A.D. 1010±60). Within this feature were not only several pieces of cordage and basketry, but the materials for their construction as well: twisted juniper bark, small willow sticks, and pine pitch (in quantities too great to be naturally occurring). Twisted juniper bark was apparently employed in the making of coarse cordage, such as artifact 5RB1463.25. Willow was evidently collected elsewhere and transported to the site for use in the construction of basketry of the type exemplified by artifact 5RB1463.58. Pine pitch is known to have been used prehistorically as a sealant for basketry (Hewitt in J. Jennings 1980:135).

Additional suppositions about the subsistence strategies and resource use of the site's various cultural groups proceed from analyses of the pollen record and recovered faunal remains. It should be noted that, since the pollen samples were taken from stratigraphic contexts (i.e., none was obtained from groundstone or coprolites), direct correlations between the pollen and economic activity cannot be drawn, although strong inferences can be made.

Economic use of three plant families is suggested by Scott's pollen analysis (Appendix C). The pollen sample from the Late Archaic level revealed a high percentage of grass pollen--almost ten times that found in samples from the Fremont and modern levels. The frequency of High-spine Compositae (sunflower) pollen was also elevated in the Late Archaic sample. Cheno-ams are fairly evenly distributed in the three cultural levels (Late Archaic, early Fremont, late Fremont), but occur three to five times more frequently in these levels than in the modern samples.

At Cowboy Cave in southeastern Utah, economic pollen analysis showed a major subsistence shift between ca 3600 B.P. and 1900 B.P. (ca. 600 B.C. and A.D. 50). Here, "grass usage appears to have shifted from about 80% to 30% while availability decreased less than 25%. Cheno-ams shifted from about 5% to more than 25%, while availability increased less than 10%." (Lindsay in J. Jennings 1980:222). This shift at Cowboy Cave may have been related to the introduction of corn (Zea) into the economic system (ibid:223). A variety of domesticated grass, corn was probably substituted into the gathering cycle; but, since the early corn was neither as productive or reliable a substitute, wild resources other than grass continued to be exploited at the usual rate with perhaps an increased reliance on later-maturing plants such as Cheno-ams. Chenopodium and amaranth are annuals that favor growth in disturbed soils and which may have been encouraged or semi-cultivated by prehistoric peoples by weeding competing plants (Gumerman 1984:153).

Late Archaic samples from the Dripping Brow site, as at Hummingbird, show relatively high frequencies of grass pollen which drop off significantly in subsequent Fremont occupations. Unlike Hummingbird, however, Dripping Brow produced small quantities of Zea in the A.D. 675, A.D. 1225, and A.D. 1550 levels (Scott in Creasman 1981:VII-44). It is probable that the introduction of maize to the Douglas Creek region occurred prior to ca. A.D. 600, causing a subsistence shift such as that at Cowboy Cave and resulting in the disparity in grass pollen between the Late Archaic and Fremont.

The burnt bone from Hummingbird Rockshelter included no large mammal specimens but only cottontail bone, implying either cultural preference or seasonality of occupation. In studies of the Anasazi at Black Mesa, hunting during the spring, summer, and early fall was largely devoted to small mammal procurement, while snowy winter months were given over to large mammal procurement as a main subsistence activity (Gumerman 1984:153-157). Assuming that wild food procurement practices differed little between the Archaic and Basketmaker/Pueblo periods (except when there may have been conflicts with planting and harvesting domesticates), it is likely that Hummingbird was also occupied during the more clement months.

Paleoclimate and Settlement Patterns in Douglas Creek

This section presents information derived from the test excavations at Hummingbird Rockshelter (5RB1463), the Brady Site (5RB726), Dripping Brow Cave (5RB695), and others in the Douglas Creek drainage and compares it with paleoenvironmental data and chronology from sites in the Four Corners area. These comparisons are made to demonstrate that the sophisticated environmental models constructed for the Colorado Plateau may apply as well to the Douglas Creek area and that the same environmental variables affected the latter's prehistoric occupation. This is not to say that the nuances of the environmental trends for the Plateau apply, but rather that the broader cycles apparently do. It is recognized, of course, that the prehistoric occupation of an area is not based exclusively on environmental variation, but on social and economic factors of the cultural groups present (Dean et al. 1985:537-538).

Paleoenvironmental models have been generated by Petersen from carbon dated peat core samples taken in the La Plata Mountains (Berry and Berry 1983:124-130) and from geological, palynological, and dendrochonological reconstructions compiled by Dean et al. (1985) for the Colorado Plateau. These models are summarized in the graphs reproduced from their original sources in Figure 16. Since the period of occupation at Hummingbird Rock-shelter extends only as far back as the Late Archaic, only the pertinent portions of the models are shown. It should be noted that little is known about high frequency environmental processes--those which effect seasonal or yearly changes--during the Archaic. Rather, researchers are reliant upon data that concern cycles longer than the human generation--low frequency processes.

Petersen and Mehringer's (1976) studies in the La Plata Mountains of southwest Colorado dated pollen from stratified bog deposits to measure fluctuations in timberline elevation for the Holocene (recent) period. The levels of arboreal pollen in samples drawn from Hummingbird are consistent with Petersen's model. From the Late Archaic level (60±70 B.C.) there is a low level of arboreal pollen relative to all others, indicative of a pro-longed dry period as shown (Figure 16A). Petersen reports a "marked con-traction of the pinyon pine forest" at this time (Berry and Berry 1983:129). In contrast, the early Fremont level at Hummingbird (A.D. 720±80) and other sites in the area shows a distinct reversal in pinyon pine forestation. In the Hummingbird sample, the ratio of pine to juniper is 5:1, while in all other of the site's samples (Late Archaic, late Fremont, modern) the ratio is 5:3. Arboreal pollen increases overall in this sample, however, and is reflective of the increased moisture prior to this date. The Hummingbird sample from A.D. 1010±60 (late Fremont) contained arboreal pollen at about the same frequency but exhibited an increased quantity of juniper and an associated decrease in pine pollen.

With respect to the model posited by Dean et al. (1985:541) shown in Figure 16B, the pine pollen from the more recent two samples from Humming-bird shows additional value as an environmental marker. Movement of pine tree populations between elevations has been shown to be reactive to low

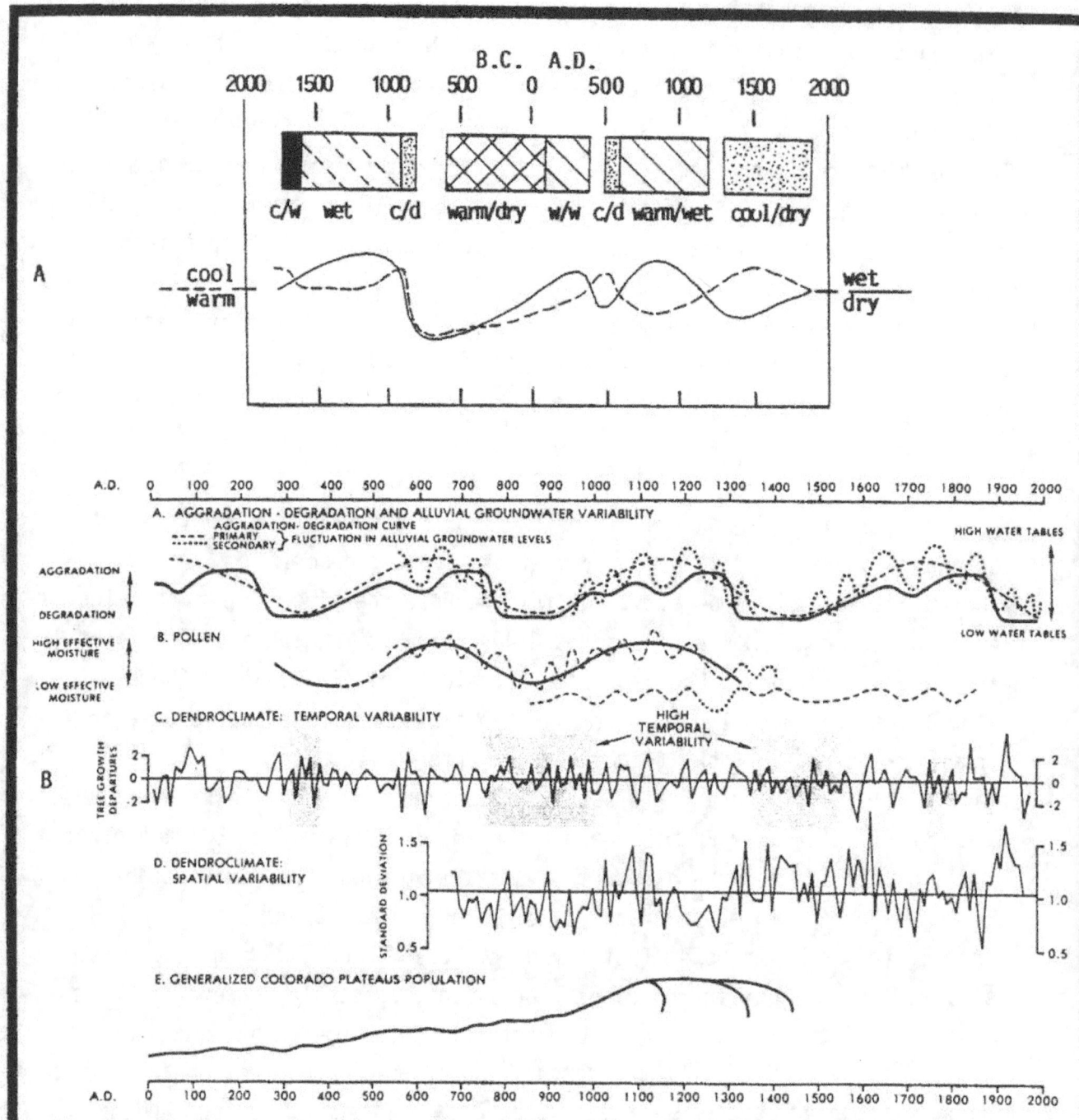

Figure 1. Environmental and demographic variability on the southern Colorado Plateaus, A.D. 1-1970. A, hydrologic fluctuations and floodplain aggradation-degradation. B, primary (solid) and secondary (dashed) fluctuations in effective moisture as indicated by pollen data. C, decadal tree growth departures in standard deviation units. D, spatial variability in dendroclimate. E, relative population trends, A.D. 1-1450.

Figure 16. Paleoenvironmental models for the La Plata Mountains (A), from Petersen in Berry and Berry 1983:126a [Figure 16]; and for the southern Colorado Plateaus (B), from Dean et al. 1985:541 [Figure 1].

frequency effective moisture cycles. It is assumed, then, that the increase in pine observed in the early Fremont sample was the direct result of increased effective moisture and possibly cooler temperatures prior to A.D. 720. The decrease in pine pollen recorded in the late Fremont sample probably reflects the period of low effective moisture that occurred over the preceding several hundred years (from which the pine forest might just be recovering). Further support of Dean et al.'s model is found in Linda Scott's pollen analyses of samples from the Brady Site (5RB726) and Dripping Brow Cave (5RB699).. Cultural levels dated ca. A.D. 650, A.D. 800, A.D. 1100, post A.D. 1220, and A.D. 1550 are described by Scott as being mesic, while sterile levels dated A.D. 115-200, A.D. 1100-1220, and post A.D. 1550 are recorded as being notably drier (Creasman 1981:VIII-43).

The comparison of pollen studies from local sites with regional models being so productive, the dates from Hummingbird Rockshelter were placed in sequence with those from the Brady Site, Dripping Brow Cave, and several others from the Douglas Creek area (Table VI, following page). After being corrected and rounded according to Damon et al. (1974), the dates were tested for contemporaneity and averaged in the manner of Long and Rippeteau (1973). Such statistical reduction of C-14 dates helps to narrow the boundaries of various occupations by reducing the quantity of dates and the statistical error (⌢) of the C-14 process. Only dates which proved to have a 50% or greater probability of contemporaneity were averaged.

A comparison of the resultant dates with those compiled by Berry (1982) in Time, Space, and Transition in Anasazi Prehistory for the period ca. 500 B.C. to A.D. 1500 on the southern Colorado Plateau was then made (Figure 17). Some interesting correlations emerged, particularly with respect to the Fremont period dates (ca. A.D. 700-1200). Berry demonstrated that there were periods of extreme rainfall deprivation and temperature increase in the Southwest which caused such hardship as to force Anasazi populations to migrate both to high elevation refugia within the Colorado Plateau and to the river drainages of the southern Basin and Range. These climatic extremes date ca. A.D. 700, 900, 1100, and 1300. Periods of marked population decline in dated Anasazi sites occur ca. A.D. 710-750, 900, 950-980,

Table VI. Radiocarbon Dates from Douglas Creek

Origin of C-14 Date	Corrected Date (Damon et al. 1974)	Averaged Date
5RB699	A.D. 1555±75	
5RB699 5RB699	A.D. 1215±65 A.D. 1205±90	A.D. 1210±55
5RB699 5RB2210	A.D. 1100±70 A.D. 1080±75	A.D. 1090±50
5RB2025 5RB1463 (Hummingbird)	A.D. 1010±65 A.D. 1010±60	A.D. 1010±45
5RB699 5RB726 5RB2449 5RB2449	A.D. 850±70 A.D. 820±70 A.D. 800±80 A.D. 780±80	A.D. 815±35 (weighted average)
5RB1463 (Hummingbird) 5RB699 5RB726	A.D. 720±80 A.D. 715±100 A.D. 675±70	A.D. 700±45 (weighted average)
5RB2449	A.D. 440±65	
5RB726	A.D. 320±70	
5RB699	A.D. 220±55	
5RB726	A.D. 195±275	
5RB699	A.D. 105±95	
5RB2212 5RB1463 (Hummingbird)	15±80 B.C. 60±70 B.C.	40±50 B.C.
5RB1463 (Hummingbird)	315±130 B.C.	

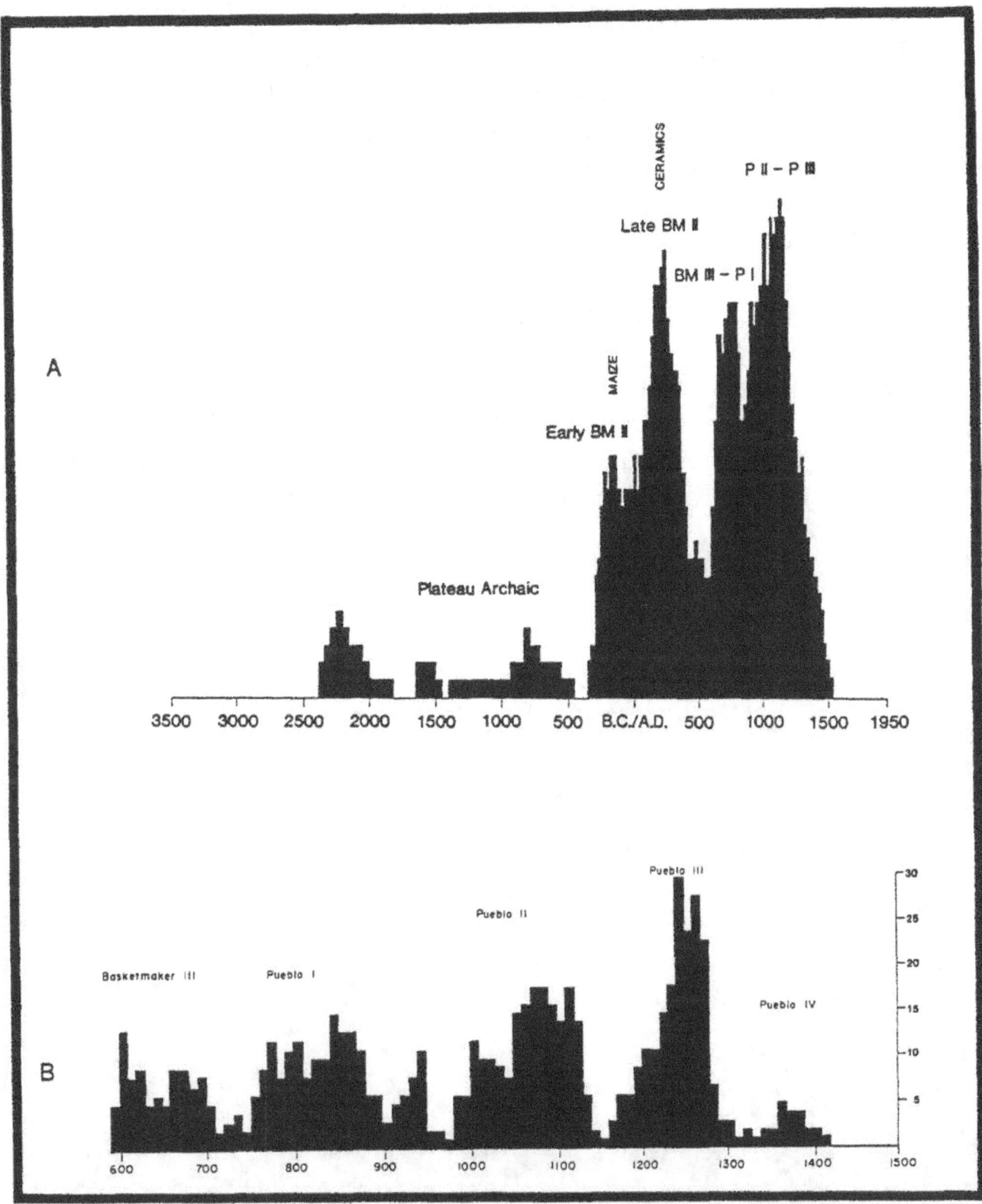

Figure 17.   Radiocarbon cultural chronology for the southern Colorado Plateau (A) and tree-ring dated sites for the period A.D. 580-1500.
(From Berry 1982:121 [Figure 20] and 105 [Figure 13B].)

1140-1160, 1280-1360, and 1380-1420 (Berry 1982:104-105). The C-14 dates from the Douglas Creek area generally cluster during the same time periods that were favorable to Anasazi tenancy of their Colorado Plateau homeland; none of the averaged dates from Douglas Creek falls within a period of decline in Anasazi occupation. Probably of equal importance are the hiatuses between the clusters of the averaged Douglas Creek dates. There appear to be significant breaks in Douglas Creek occupation between A.D. 720-780, 850-1000, 1100-1200, and 1300-1450.

The Late Archaic period dates were also compared with Berry (ibid: 120-121). The greatest low points in C-14 dates for the southern Colorado Plateau during this time occur ca. 450-350 B.C. and A.D. 450-600. The greatest numbers of recorded dates occur ca. 250 B.C. and A.D. 200. None of the Douglas Creek dates falls within either hiatus and, in general, there is a positive correspondence of dates to peaks in Berry's C-14 bar graph for the southern Plateau.

MANAGEMENT SUMMARY

The Hummingbird Rockshelter, site 5RB1463, was officially determined eligible for inclusion in the National Register of Historic Places (NRHP) by agreement between the Colorado State Historic Preservation officer and the Bureau of Land Management (BLM). The site was considered significant because of its potential to yield scientific data concerning the cultural prehistory of the Douglas Creek area.

With the completion of this study, the stipulations set forth by the BLM concerning the mitigation of the vandal's impacts to the site have been met by Beartooth Oil and Gas Company. A determination of no adverse effect as mandated by 36 CFR 800.4(c) is provided.

The Hummingbird Rockshelter yielded significant information about the Late Archaic and Fremont occupations of the Douglas Creek area. Research questions generated by this work include: When did Zea (corn) appear in the area and what effect did it have on the subsistence strategies of resident groups? Did permanent settlement in Douglas Creek occur during the Fremont period (A.D. 400-1200)? Or did it occur later? How did climatic variation affect settlement patterns, i.e. were rockshelters occupied mostly during moderately dry periods and open campsites during wet periods? Was there complete abandonment during extreme drought(s)?

It is hoped that future research in the Douglas Creek area may allow some of these questions to be answered and contribute to further refinement of the prehistoric record in northwestern Colorado.

REFERENCES

Adovasio, J.M.
   1980   Fremont: An artifactual perspective. In Fremont Perspectives, edited by David B. Madsen. Utah State Historical Society Antiquities Section Selected Papers 7 (16):35-40.

Berry, Claudia F. and Michael S. Berry
   1983   Chronological and Conceptual Models of the Southwestern Archaic. (unpublished manuscript)

Berry, Michael S.
   1982   Time, Space, and Transition in Anasazi Prehistory. University of Utah Press, Salt Lake City.

Breternitz, David A.
   1970   Archaeological excavations in Dinosaur National Monument, Colorado-Utah, 1964-1965. University of Colorado Studies Series in Anthropology No. 17, Boulder.

Bureau of Land Management
   1978   Unit resource analysis - Rangely planning unit. Craig District Office, Craig.

Burgh, Robert F.
   1948   The archaeology of Castle Park, Dinosaur National Monument. University of Colorado Studies, Series in Anthropology No. 2, Boulder.

Conner, Carl E. and Diana L. Langdon
   1980   Cultural resources inventory, federal sodium lease C--118326. Report prepared for MultiMineral Corporation. Grand River Institute, Grand Junction.

Conner, Carl E.; Diana L. Langdon; and Richard W. Ott
   1980   Cultural resources inventory of the Grand Valley gas play mainline gathering system for Southwest Gathering Company, Inc. Grand River Institute, Grand Junction.

Creasman, Steven D.
   1981   Archaeological investigations in the Canyon Pintado Historic District, Rio Blanco County, Colorado. Phase I - inventory and test excavations. Reports of LOPA No. 34, Colorado State University, Fort Collins.

Damon, P.E.; C.W. Ferguson; A. Long; and E.I. Wallick
   1974   Dendrochronologic calibration of the radiocarbon time scale. American Antiquity 39(2):351-366.

Dean, Jeffery S.; Robert C. Euler; George J. Gumerman; Fred Plog; Richard H. Hevly; and Thor N.V. Karlstrom
   1985   Human behavior, demography, and paleoenvironment on the Colorado Plateaus. American Antiquity 50(3):537-554.

Frison, George C.
   1978   Prehistoric Hunters of the High Plains. Academic Press, New York.

Gooding, John D.
     1981   The archaeology of Vail Pass camp. Highway Salvage Report
            No. 35. Colorado Department of Highways and University of
            Colorado Museum, Boulder.

Gordon, E. Kinzie; Kris J. Kranzush; Donna J. Knox; Victoria E. Keen;
            and Craig A. Engleman
     1981   A class III cultural inventory of the Texas-Missouri-Evacua-
            tion Creeks study area, Rio Blanco County, Colorado. Report
            prepared for the Bureau of Land Management. Gordon & Kran-
            zush, Boulder.

Grady, James
     1984   Northwest Colorado prehistoric context. The State Historical
            Society of Colorado, Denver.

Gumerman, George J.
     1984   A View from Black Mesa, the Changing Face of Archaeology. Uni-
            versity of Arizona Press, Tucson.

Hewitt, Nancy J.
     1980   The occurrence of pinyon pine at Cowboy Cave. In Cowboy Cave,
            by Jesse D. Jennings. University of Utah Anthropological Pa-
            pers No. 104, Salt Lake City.

Holmer, Richard N. and Dennis G. Weder
     1980   Common post-Archaic projectile points of the Fremont area. In
            Fremont Perspectives, edited by David B. Madsen. Utah State
            Historical Society Antiquities Section Selected Papers No. 7
            (16):55-68.

Jennings, Jesse D.
     1978   Prehistory of Utah and the eastern Great Basin. University of
            Utah Anthropological Papers No. 98, Salt Lake City.

Lindsay, LaMar W.
     1980   Pollen analysis of Cowboy Cave cultural deposits. In Cowboy
            Cave, by Jesse D. Jennings. University of Utah Anthropologi-
            cal Papers No. 104, Salt Lake City.

Lister, Robert H.
     1951   Excavation at Hell's Midden, Dinosaur National Monument. Uni-
            versity of Colorado Studies Series in Anthropology No. 3,
            Boulder.

Long, Austin and Bruce Rippeteau
     1974   Testing contemporaneity and averaging radiocarbon dates. Amer-
            ican Antiquity 39(2):205-215.

Madsen, David B. and Michael S. Berry
     1975   A reassessment of northeastern Great Basin prehistory. American
            Antiquity 40(4):391-405.

Martin, Gary; Donna C. Daniels; and Penny J. McPherson
     1980   A cultural resource inventory of a core hole and access road re-
            location for MultiMineral Corporation in Rio Blanco County, Colo-
            rado. Western Cultural Resource Management, Inc., Meeker.

Olsen, Larry D.
  1973   Outdoor Survival Skills. Fourth edition. Brigham Young Uni-
          versity Press, Provo.

Petersen, Kenneth p. and Peter J. Mehringer, Jr.
  1976   Postglacial timberline fluctuations, La Plata Mountains, south-
          west Colorado. Arctic and Alpine Research 8(3):275-288.

Redman, Charles L.
  1975   Productive sampling strategies for archaeological sites. In
          Sampling in Archaeology, James W. Mueller, editor.

Scott, Linda J.
  1981   Pollen analysis of two sites in the Canyon Pintado Historic
          District, Rio Blanco County, Colorado. Appendix F in Archaeo-
          logical investigations in the Canyon Pintado Historic District,
          Rio Blanco County, Colorado, by Steven D. Creasman. Reports
          of LOPA No. 34, Colorado State University, Fort Collins.

  1983   Paleoenvironmental interpretations in the Douglas Creek drain-
          age. Appendix 1 in Final report on the archaeological moni-
          toring of Northwest Pipeline Corporation's trunk "d" pipe-
          line in the Canyon Pintado Historic District, by Steven D.
          Creasman. Cultural Resources Management Report No. 9.
          Archaeological Services, Western Wyoming College, Rock Springs.

Smith, Anne M.
  1974   Ethnography of the northern Utes. Museum of New Mexico Papers
          in Anthropology No. 17, Albuquerque.

Steward, Julian H.
  1974   Ute Indians I. Garland Publishers, New York.

Stucky, Richard K.
  1977   The Sand Wash Basin, northwestern Colorado. Master's thesis,
          Department of Anthropology, University of Colorado, Boulder.

Wenger, Gilbert
  1956   An archaeological survey of Southern Blue Mountain and Douglas
          Creek in northwestern Colorado. Master's thesis, Department
          of Anthropology, University of Denver.

APPENDIX A

(Archaeomagnetic Analysis by J. Holly Hathaway)

Department of Anthropology
Archaeomagnetic Laboratory

Colorado State University
Fort Collins, Colorado
80523

June 20, 1985

Carl E. Conner
Grand River Institute
P.O. Box 3543
Grand Junction, Colorado 81502

Dear Carl,

Enclosed please find the results of the archaeomagnetic sample collected from site 5RB1463. Unfortunately, the sample was not sufficiently magnetized to obtain a consistent, strong direction for dating. Generally, we have found that samples with excessive sand content do not work out for archaeomagnetic dating. This is especially true for features located in cliff dwellings or overhangs where there is no clay material brought in to make a clay collar around the hearth/feature.

As I mentioned on the telephone last week, there will be no charge for the analysis of the sample. If you find other features this summer, please give me a call and we will discuss the possibility of collecting the sample(s). It sounds as though you may be excavating some features worth discussing in the near future.

Sincerely,

J. Holly Hathaway
Laboratory Associate

ARCHAEOMAGNETIC LABORATORY REPORT

Archaeomagnetic Laboratory
Department of Anthropology
Colorado State University
Ft. Collins, Colorado 80521
(303) 491-5784 or 491-7408

Sample I.D. __5RB1463-1__   Feature I.D. __Feature 1__

Site Latitude __39.87°N__   Site Longitude __251.24°E__   Site Declination __13.0°E__

Collector __J. H. Hathaway__   Date Collected __06-04-85__   Archaeological Guess Date __AD 700-900__

Laboratory Analysis

Demagnetization Steps (Oersteds)	NRM				
Alpha 95 (degrees)	26.15				
Precision Parameter (k)	3.72				
Inclination (degrees)	69.46				
Declination (degrees)	309.09				
Mean Sample Intensity (x10^{-3} emu/cc)	.0067				
No. Specimens Collected/ No. Specimens Used	12/12				
Outliers	-				

Final Processing Results

Sample Measurement:

NRM	Demagnetization Level Used
53.44	Paleolatitude (degrees North)
199.85	Paleolongitude (degrees East)
38.19	Error along the great circle (EP)
44.69	Error perpendicular to the great circle (EM)

Comments:

Due to the very large alpha 95 value obtained at the NRM level and the associated low level of magnetic remanent intensity, this sample was not demagnetized. No plot or date are provided for the sample.

Signed: _J. Hoy Hathaway_   Date: 6/20/85

APPENDIX B

(Radiocarbon Analysis by Beta Analytic Inc.)

BETA ANALYTIC INC.

RADIOCARBON DATING, STABLE ISOTOPE RATIOS, THERMOLUMINESCENCE, X-RAY DIFFRACTION
P. O. BOX 248113   CORAL GABLES, FLORIDA 33124   (305) 667-5167

Dr. Danni L. Langdon   July 16, 1985
Grand River Institute
P.O. Box 3543
Grand Junction, CO   31502

Dear Dr. Langdon:

    Please find enclosed our report on the four charcoal samples
that you recently submitted for radiocarbon dating analyses. We
hope the dates fulfill appropriate expectations.

    Each of the charcoals were good material and of appropriate
size for dating. #0 was borderline in size but we felt that ex-
tended counter time probably wasn't necessary. Each charcoal was
first visually examined and carefully picked for rootlets or any
other noncontemporaneous carbonaceous materials. They were then
subjected to an alternating series of hot acid and alkali solutions
to remove any groundwater carbonates or humic acids. These were
interspersed with rinsings in hot distilled water, ending with a
gentle drying. This was followed by chemical conversion and measurement of radioactivity levels. All pretreatment and analysis
steps proceeded normally.

    Our statement is enclosed. Would you please forward it to the
appropriate office for payment. Thank you for the nice compliments-
they are appreciated by all. If you have any questions and would
like to confer on the dates, please don't hesitate to call us at
any time.

                                        Sincerely yours,

                                        Jerry Stipp

                                        Jerry J. Stipp, PhD
                                        Co-director

JJS/hs
Encl: report, statement, extra Sx data sheets.

P.S. Also subtlely enclosed is one genuine Beta field cap for you
protection, and sartorial splendor.

BETA ANALYTIC INC.

UNIVERSITY BRANCH
P.O. BOX 248113
CORAL GABLES, FLA. 33124

(305) 667-5167

REPORT OF RADIOCARBON DATING ANALYSES

FOR: Dr. Danni L. Langdon

Grand River Institute

Grand Junction, CO

DATE RECEIVED: June 25, 1985

DATE REPORTED: July 16, 1985

BILLED TO SUBMITTER'S
INVOICE NUMBER ___ letter of 6/20/85

OUR LAB NUMBER	YOUR SAMPLE NUMBER	C-14 AGE YEARS B.P. ± 1σ	Material
Beta-13039	#0	2,220 ± 90	charcoal
Beta-13040	#6	940 ± 50	"
Beta-13041	GRI 8512 - 10	1,250 ± 60	"
Beta-13042	GRI 8512 -14	2,000 ± 60	"

APPENDIX C

(Pollen Analysis by Linda J. Scott)

POLLEN ANALYSIS OF 5RB1463, AN OVERHANG CONTAINING
LATE ARCHAIC AND FREMONT DEPOSITS

By
Linda J. Scott
Palynological Analysts
Golden, Colorado

Prepared for

Grand River Institute
Grand Junction, Colorado 81502

October 1985

INTRODUCTION

Site 5RB1463 is located on a terrace overlooking Little Bull Draw at an elevation of 6240' in a pinyon/juniper community. Five pollen samples were taken at this site in an effort to define the paleoenvironment and possibly also obtain subsistence data. Radiocarbon dates ranging from 940±50 B.P. to 2220±90 B.P. were returned for two features, indicating both Fremont and Late Archaic occupation of the site.

METHODS

The pollen was extracted from soil samples submitted by Grand River Institute from 5RB1463. A chemical extraction technique based on flotation is the standard preparation technique used in this laboratory for the removal of the pollen from the large volume of sand, silt, and clay with which they are mixed. This particular process was developed for extraction of pollen from soils where preservation has been less than ideal and pollen density is low.

Hydrochloric acid (10%) was used to remove calcium carbonates present in the soil, after which the samples were screened through 150 micron mesh. Zinc bromide (density 2.0) was used for the flotation process. All samples received a short (10 minute) treatment in hot hydrofluoric acid to remove any remaining inorganic particles. The samples were then acetolated for three minutes to remove any extraneous organic matter.

A light microscope was used to count the pollen to a total of 200 to 400 pollen grains at a magnification of 430x. Pollen preservation in these samples varied from excellent to good. Comparative reference material collected at the Intermountain Herbarium at Utah State University and the University of Colorado Herbarium was used to identify the pollen to the family, genus, and species level, where possible.

TABLE 1. POLLEN COUNT FROM 5RB1463 (HUMMINGBIRD ROCKSHELTER)

Scientific Name	Common Name	Sample 1 No.	Sample 1 %	Sample 2 No.	Sample 2 %	Sample 4 No.	Sample 4 %	Sample 5 No.	Sample 5 %	Sample 7 No.	Sample 7 %
ABOREAL POLLEN:											
Abies	Fir										
Betula	Birch	37	18.5	1	.25	1	0.5			1	0.5
Juniperus	Juniper			99	24.75	31	15.5	128	31.3	16	8.0
Picea												
Pinus	Pine	60	30.0	203	50.75	50	25.0	185	45.25	86	43.0
Pseudotsuga	Douglas fir							1	0.25		
Quercus	Oak	1	0.5	6	1.50	2	1.0	4	1.9	5	2.5
Salix	Willow							1	0.25		
Cheno-ams	Includes amaranth & pigweed family	51	25.5	17	4.25	53	26.5	9	2.2	35	17.5
Sarcobatus	Greasewood	3	1.5	6	1.5			6	1.7	1	0.5
Compositae:	Sunflower family										
Artemisia	Sagebrush	35	17.5	37	9.25	15	7.5	41	10.0	35	17.5
Low-spine	Includes ragweed, cocklebur, etc.	1	0.5	7	1.75	9	4.5	11	.2.7	5	2.5
High-spine	Includes aster, rabbitbrush, sunflower	7	3.5	7	1.75	13	6.5	7	1.5	9	4.5
Cruciferae	Mustard family	1	0.5					5	1.2		
Cyperaceae	Sedge family							1	0.25		
Ephedra nevadensis	Mormon tea	1	0.5	5	1.25			2	0.5		
Ephedra torreyana	Mormon tea							1	0.25		
Eriogonum	Wild buckwheat			1	0.25	1	0.5				
Gramineae	Grass family	3	1.5	10	2.50	20	10.0	2	0.5	2	1.0
Rosaceae	Rose family					1	0.5	1	0.25	1	0.5
Cercocarpus	Mt. mahogany							1	0.25	2	1.0
Saxifragaceae											
Shepherdia	Buffaloberry			1	0.25	1	0.5			1	0.5
Solanaceae	Tomato/potato fam.										
Indeterminate						3	1.5	3	0.75	2	1.0
Total Pollen Grains		200	100.0	400	100.0	200	100.0	409	100.0	200	200.0

DISCUSSION

Site 5RB1463 is situated in a pinyon/juniper community on a terrace overlooking Little Bull Draw at an elevation of 6240'. The site is located in a shallow overhang, which afforded protection to portions of the sediments. Five pollen samples were taken from this site, and represent: a mixed soil and bark layer at the back of the overhang (10N6W), 17-22cm below the surface from a level that was radiocarbon dated to 940±50 B.P. (Sample 1); the present ground surface (3N2E) (Sample 2); a dark ash and charcoal level (8N6W) 28-36cm below the present ground surface that radiocarbon dated to 2000±60 B.P. (Sample 4); a level (10N6W) 3-8cm below the surface which may contain modern pollen (Sample 5); and an ashy layer (10N6W) approximately 22-29cm below the surface that radiocarbon dated to 1250±60 B.P. (Sample 7).

The pollen record from this site displays large frequencies of both Juniperus and Pinus pollen at the present ground surface and immediately below the present ground surface (Samples 2 and 5 respectively). The pollen frequencies observed in these samples are consistent with those expected given the present vegetation. Arboreal pollen frequencies are noted to be variable in other pollen studies in the Douglas Creek drainage (Scott 1981). Stratigraphic analysis of sediments on a knoll at the mouth of Vandamore Draw yielded evidence of large quantities of arboreal pollen at the present, and extending back to before A.D. 780 (Scott 1980).

Samples 1 and 7, representing two different periods of Fremont occupation at the site, contain pollen more similar to one another than to either of the samples from the modern vegetation community. The two contain similar quantities of arboreal pollen, although Sample 1 (940±50 B.P.) from the later Fremont occupation exhibits a larger quantity of juniper pollen and a lesser frequency of pine pollen than does Sample 7 (1250±60 B.P.), representing the earlier Fremont. The large quantity of pine pollen observed in Sample 7 corresponds well to dated levels elsewhere in the Douglas Creek drainage exhibiting elevated Pinus pollen frequencies, including that at Vandamore Draw dated to A.D. 780 (Scott 1983). Both Samples 1 and

7 contain relatively high Cheno-am pollen frequencies, which may reflect either an increase in one or more members of this group of plants in the local environment (possibly due to ground disturbance) or the utilization of Cheno-ams during both periods of occupation. The nature of the deposit representing the later Fremont occupation at the back of the overhang suggests, however, that the first interpretation is the more likely. Cheno-ams are weedy annuals that grow well in disturbed conditions. They have been frequently exploited for both their greens, which are used as a potherb, and their seeds, which may be ground into meal (Chamberlin 1915; Gilmore 1977; Harrington 1967; Palmer 1871; Rogers 1980; Whiting 1939).

Pollen Sample #4, representing the Archaic occupation, was radiocarbon dated to 2000±60 B.P. This sample contains less arboreal pollen than either of the Fremont samples (the difference being primarily in the quantity of Pinus pollen), suggesting that the local pine population was diminished compared with that in evidence during the Fremont occupation. This may have been due to slightly drier and/or warmer conditions during the Archaic. The quantity of Cheno-am pollen present in Sample #4 is very similar to that present observed in the Fremont levels and may represent an increased population of saltbush during both the Archaic and Fremont occupations compared with that of the present. The large quantity of Gramineae (grass) pollen and the presence of aggregates of grass pollen in this sample may be the result of economic activity; the frequencies are considerably higher than those observed in other samples from this site. Grass seeds may be collected and ground into meal for consumption (Harrington 1967), and grasses are useful in lining cooking pits and in making mats. An elevated frequency of High-spine Compositae pollen, as well as aggregates of this pollen type, suggest that a member of this family may have been used economically as well. Helianthus (sunflower) is frequently exploited for its seeds.

SUMMARY AND CONCLUSIONS

The slight differences in pollen frequencies between the three samples representing late and early Fremont and Late Archaic occupations of this site indicate that the local invironment did not vary significantly during those occupations from that of today. The area in the immediate vicinity of the site appears to have been slightly more open and perhaps also slightly warmer and/or drier than present. This is suggested by the decrease in arboreal pollen compared with that exhibited in the samples containing modern pollen and by the increase in Cheno-am pollen in the three cultural samples (Samples 1, 4, and 7). The peak of pine pollen observed at 1250±60 B.P. correlates well with peaks of increased pine pollen in the Douglas Creek area, and may represent short-lived, mesic and/or cooler conditions. A large quantity of Gramineae pollen recorded in the sample from the Late Archaic (2000±60 B.P.) may indicate economic use of grass.

REFERENCES CITED

Chamberlin, Ralph V.
    1915   The Ethnobotany of the Gosiute Indians of Utah. American
            Anthropological Association Memoirs, 2:329-405.

Gilmore, Melvin R.
    1977   Uses of Plants by the Indians o the Missouri River Region.
            Reprinted, University of Nebraska Press, Lincoln. Originally
            published 1915, Bureau of American Ethnology, Washington, D.C.

Harrington, H. D.
    1967   Edible Native Plants of the Rocky Mountains. University of New
            Mexico Press, Albuquerque.

Palmer, Edward
    1871   Food Products of the North American Indians. In Report of the
            Commissioner of Agriculture for 1870, edited by J. R. Dodge, pp.
            404:428. U. S. Government Printing Office, Washington D.C.

Rogers, Dilwyn
    1980   Edible, Medicinal, Useful, and Poisonous Wild Plants of the
            Northern Great Plains--South Dakota Region. Biology Department,
            Augustana College, Sioux Falls, South Dakota.

Scott, Linda J.
    1981   Pollen Analysis of Two Sites in the Canyon Pintado Historic
            District, Rio Blanco County, Colorado. Appendix F IN
            Archaeological Investigations in the Canyon Pintado Historic
            District, Rio Blanco County, Colorado, Phase I - Inventory and
            Test Excavations by Steven D. Creasman. Reports of the Laboratory
            of Public Archaeology No. 34. Laboratory of Public Archaeology,
            Colorado State University, Fort Collins.

            1983   Paleoenvironmental Interpretations in the Douglas Creek
            Drainage. Appendix 1 IN Final Report on the Archaeological
            Monitoring of Northwest Pipeline Corporation's Trunk "D" Pipeline
            in the Canyon Pintado Historic District by Steven D. Creasman.
            Cultural Resources Management Report No. 9. Archaeological
            Services, Western Wyoming College, Rock Springs.

Whiting, Alfred F.
    1939   Ethnobotany of the Hopi. Museum of Northern Arizona Bulletin No.
            15. Flagstaff.

APPENDIX D
(Faunal Analysis by Elaine Anderson)

5 August 1985

Carl Conner
Grand River Institute
P.O. Box 3543
Grand Junction, CO 81502

Dear Carl,

Here are the faunal identifications for 5RB1463 and Little Bull Draw.
Sorry I didn't get them back to you before this. Last week I got the galley
proofs of my ferret monograph to check over carefully and everything else was
put aside.

Lots of fragmentary rabbit bones (many burned) from 1463 as well as prairie
dog, fence lizard mummies, a frog/toad pelvis and some insect pupa cases. The
dung samples include canid (probably coyote), sheep, large bovid (cow/bison)
and probably deer. The partial skeleton of the gray fox from Little Bull Draw
is very nice - they are uncommon in faunas. The mandible belonged to a domestic
cat.

I spent 4 hours on this project = 4 hrs. @ $8.00/hr. = $32.00.

Thank you for contacting me for faunal identification. I'll be glad to
help you with any other faunal material you find. Under separate cover, I'm
returning the bones you sent me.

Sincerely yours,

Elaine

Elaine Anderson
730 Magnolia St.
Denver, CO 80220

Rio Blanco Co. Little Bull Draw - approx. 6200' elevation. CWM 6/5/85

Fauna

<u>Urocyon</u> <u>cinereoargenteus</u> - Gray Fox (Recent) - juvenile

R anterior half of skull w/ C, P^4-M^1

L anterior half of skull w/ C, P^{1-4} assoc.

posterior 2/3 skull (sutures open)

jaw symphysis w/ R I_{1-3}, C, P_1-M_2; L I_{1-3}, C, P_{1-2}, P_4-M_1 (no alveolus for P_3)

L scapula

L humerus (proximal epiphsis lost)   assoc.

L ulna

L radius

5 thoracic vertebrae

lumbar vertebra

8 ribs

Rio Blanco Co. Douglas Creek

<u>Felis</u> <u>catus</u> - Domestic Cat

L jaw w/ C, P_3-M_1

Fauna

10N 7W   5-26 cm   F.S. 75

    Sylvilagus sp. - Cottontail

        distal end of L tibia

9N 6W   20-30 cm   F.S. 12

    Sylvilagus sp. - Cottontail

        frag. prox. end of tibia

        4 frags. long bones (burned)

    Indet. medium-sized mammal

        2 frags.

9N 6W   20-30 cm   F.S. 12

    Sylvilagus sp.- Cottontail

        2 frags. lng bone (1 burned)

    Indet. small mammal

        2 frags. long bone

9N 6W   40-50 cm   F.S. 18

    Sylvilagus sp. - Cottontail

        frag. long bone (burned)

7N 6W 1-14 cm   F.S. 3I

    Sylvilagus sp. - Cottontail

        frag. L jaw w/M_3 (broken)

        2 frags. long bones (1 burned)

7N 6W   0-40 cm   F.S. 38

    Sylvilagus sp. - Cottontail

        4 frags long bones (all burned)

8N 11W 0-16 cm   F.S. 49

    Sylvilagus sp. - Cottontail (fetal)

        4 skull frags.

        L ulna

        frag. of ilium

        prox. end of tibia

        prox. end of humerus

    Sylvilagus sp. - Cottontail (adult)

        frag. vertebra

        2 frags. long bone

    Amphibian - Frog or toad

        ilium of pelvis

Fauna

10N 6W 5-33 cm F.S. 39, 44, 66, 80

    Sylvilagus sp. - Cottontail

        R scapula

        frag. of scapula

        dist. end of R humerus

        midsect. radius

        2 complete ribs

        3 rib frags.

        7 frags. long bones

    Cynomys leucurus - White-tailed Prairie Dog

        dist. end L tibia

        dist. end of fibula

        2 frags. long bones

10N 6W 25-33 cm

    cf Sylvilagus - Cottontail

        frag. long bone (burned)

Vandals backdirt pile

    Sylvilagus sp. - Cottontail

        frag. of scapula

        frag. of ilium

        prox. end MT III

        12 frags. long bones (8 burned)

10N 7W 5-26 cm

    Insecta

        6 empty pupal cases

    Indet. small mammal

        mass of hair

        middle phalanx (embedded in hair)

10N 6W 5-22 cm F.S. 39, 44, 66, 80

    Sceloporus undulatus - Western Fence Lizard

        5 mummies (4 juveniles)

7N 7W 1-25 cm F.S. 78

    Sylvilagus sp. - Cottontail

        frag. of scapula

8N 7W 2-25 cm F.S. 68

    cf Sylvilagus - Cottontail

        3 frags (2 burned)

Fauna

8N 7W 25-45 cm F.S. 73

    Indet. small mammal

        1 frag. (burned)

8N 7W 25-45 cm F.S. 72

    Land Snail

        3 small shell frags.

10N 7W 5-26 cm F.S. 75

    <u>Sylvilagus</u> sp. - Cottontail

        dist. end R tibia

        2 midsects. tibiae

        2 midsects. ulnae

        5 frags. long bones (all burned)

10N 6W 1-16 cm F.S. 40

    Mammal dung

        Canid cf coyote containing rabbit hair

        cf domestic sheep

        bovid - cow/bison

        cf deer

10N 7W 0-15 cm

    Mammal dung

        Canid cf coyote containing rabbit hair, bones of <u>Sylvilagus</u> = ulna

            and frag. of scapula

        sheep pellets

        cf cow turds

www.ingramcontent.com/pod-product-compliance
Lightning Source LLC
Chambersburg PA
CBHW080321290526
45790CB00005B/2137